A Pictorial History
of Benton County

Corvallis Gazette-Times
Benton County Historical Society and Museum

ACKNOWLEDGEMENTS

For more information regarding the
History of Benton County, please contact:

Benton County Historical Society and Museum
P.O. Box 35
Philomath, Oregon 97370-0035
Phone (541) 929-6230
Fax (541) 929-6261

ISBN 1-56037-175-7

Project Coordinator, Gazette-Times:
Amy Callahan

Introductions and captions compiled by:
Mary Gallagher
Judy Juntunen
Lawrence A. Landis

Corvallis Gazette-Times
600 S.W. Jefferson
Corvallis, OR 97333
www.gtconnect.com

Printed in Canada

Photos Submitted by:
- Robert Adams
- Dean Almgren
- Lou Baxter
- Robert Blackledge
- Dorothy Brown
- Judy Ann Butler
- Maxine (Hunter) Byler
- Irene Childears
- Margaret Coon
- Rob Corl
- Lisa Curtis
- Lorraine Dougherty
- John Dougherty
- Susan Fields
- Marlene Furman
- Gerding Family
- Theodore Gump
- Barbara Hays
- Alvah Hinton
- Patti Janego
- George and Rita Johnson
- Robert R. Lowry
- Jean Mater
- Vernetta McCallum
- Marlene McDonald
- Julian McFadden
- Sheldon M. Meier
- Barbara Metzger
- Linda Olsen
- Velma Rawie
- Joe Rictor
- Kathryn R. Schultz
- George Stovall
- Elmer Taylor
- Amy Edwards Weideman
- Virginia C. Weir

The Benton County Historical Society and Museum
Oregon State University Archives
The Wren Historical Society

With Special Thanks to:
The Benton County Historical Society and Museum
  Mary Gallagher
  Judy Juntunen
  Bill Lewis
Farcountry Press
  Brad Hurd, Publisher
  Kathy Springmeyer, Production Manager
  Barbara Fifer, Special Projects Editor
  Bob Smith, Graphic Designer
The Gazette-Times
  Debbie Pierce
Oregon State University Archives
  Lawrence A. Landis
  Elizabeth Nielsen
The Wren Historical Society
  Karen Kennedy

A Pictorial history
of Benton County

Table of
Contents

A BRIEF HISTORY OF

BENTON COUNTY

THE KALAPUYA

Before the arrival of explorers, fur trappers, and settlers, the Willamette Valley looked much different from the way it looks today. The Willamette River and its main tributaries were lined with trees growing closely together in corridors from one-fourth to three miles wide. Water levels changed with the seasons, and the low-lying areas often flooded—creating lakes, ponds, and marshes. Wapato grew in these swampy areas. Camas and tall grasses grew on the prairies, and berries grew in the mountains. Fish were abundant in the rivers and streams, and game was plentiful in the valley and in the nearby mountains.

Image from the *Narrative of the United States Exploring Expedition During the Years 1838, 1839, 1840, 1842* by Charles Wilkes, USN. LEA & BLANCHARD 1845.

With the use of deliberate fires, the Kalapuya, the indigenous people of the area, maintained the valley floor as wide, open prairies with tall grasses. Without this annual burning, the valley floor would have been densely covered with trees. As a result of these fires, only scattered groves of trees dotted the prairies on the valley floor. In the early 1800s, the Kalapuya inhabited a rich, green land of plenty.

The Kalapuya spoke four languages and eight dialects derived from the same language family—Kalapuyan-Takelman. Anthropologists divide the Kalapuya into bands based on these language differences. Historians believe that each band had at least one member who could understand and translate the languages of nearby bands. Collectively, the Native Americans who lived in present-day Oregon spoke at least twenty-one languages and forty dialects.

It is not known how many bands existed. Estimates of population for the Kalapuya range from 14,000 to 20,000. A typical band—fifty to one hundred people—was made up of several families, which spent the winter months in a main year-around village. In the spring through the fall, members usually split into smaller family units, establishing seasonal camps for harvesting plant foods, hunting game, and fishing.

A band had one or two headmen, who often were the wealthiest members. Another important person was a spiritual leader or shaman, who could be either a woman or a man. Believed to possess great supernatural powers, the shamans could cure the sick, and they also were expected to find the reasons and solutions for community problems.

Life for the Kalapuya changed dramatically after Euroamericans came to the Willamette Valley. Many of the Kalapuya died from diseases introduced by the newcomers. By 1856, nearly all the remaining Native Americans in western Oregon had been forced to move onto reservations either at Grand Ronde or Siletz. Today, some of the descendants of these Kalapuya still live in western Oregon.

THE FIRST SETTLERS

The first non-native people to settle in Benton County arrived in 1845. Benton County was established on December 23, 1847, as the seventh county organized in territorial Oregon. Its western border stretched to the Pacific Ocean, and its southern border to what is now the boundary between Oregon and California. In 1851, as other counties were established, Benton County's southern border was set at its approximate present boundary, but its western boundary was still the Pacific Ocean.

By the 1890s, people living in the western part of the county were dissatisfied being so far from the county seat, Corvallis, and felt that the county government was unresponsive to their needs. It took at least a week to travel back and forth to get business done. So they asked the legislature to create a new county. Corvallis residents spent $5,000 in an effort to keep Benton County intact, but in 1893 Lincoln County was created. Compared to other Oregon counties, Benton County is currently ranked third smallest in total size, encompassing 679 square miles in the heart of the Willamette Valley, although it is the ninth largest in population.

Benton County was named in honor of Senator Thomas Hart Benton (1782-1858) of Missouri, a strong advocate of free land laws. He was the first senator from Missouri, and the first U.S. Senator to serve thirty years in Congress (1820-1851). His support for American farmers and westward expansion of the United States helped lead to the growth and development of Oregon. Along with Lewis Linn, the junior senator from Missouri, Benton pushed through the Oregon Donation Land Act, which essential-

ly gave settlers free land if they met certain requirements. The act allowed the most generous land distribution in United States history. Of course, the land was not the property of the United States—it still belonged to the Native Americans. With some treaties after the fact, the United States acquired ownership.

One of the first settlers in the Corvallis area was Joseph C. Avery, who arrived in 1845. He settled on the north side of the Marys River near the confluence of the Marys and Willamette. During the winter of 1847-1848, he marked twelve acres of land around his cabin for town lots and, in February 1851, Avery platted the Town of Marysville on his claim. William F. Dixon platted Dixon's Addition to the town on his claim directly north of Avery's. In that same year, Marysville was officially named the county seat. In 1853, to avoid confusion with a city by the same name in California, Marysville was renamed Corvallis, which means "heart of the valley."

In 1855, Corvallis briefly became the capital of the Oregon Territory. One result was the publication of the first newspaper in Corvallis, the *Oregon Statesman*. Many citizens were concerned about permanently moving the capital to Corvallis, because there was a question about whether this had to be approved by Congress. What were Oregonians going to do with a partially constructed territorial capitol in Salem, built with money appropriated by Congress? In December, the Legislature met in a two-story, wood-frame building donated by Avery on the northwest corner of Second and Adams streets. They passed one bill—a bill to move the capital back to Salem. The *Oregon Statesman* followed.

Towns in Benton County developed and prospered. Corvallis, in particular, grew quite rapidly for several reasons. Located on the navigable headwaters of the Willamette River, Corvallis developed into a regional trading center. In 1868, Corvallis College was also designated "as the Agricultural College" of the State of Oregon, a land grant college under the Morrill Act that had been signed by President Abraham Lincoln. In 1879, the development of the railroad in Corvallis spurred further growth.

Outside of Corvallis, other communities emerged, including Philomath to the west, Monroe, Alpine, and Bellfountain in the southern part of the county, Alsea in the Southwest, and Blodgett, Wren, Kings Valley, and Summit in the northwest. Adair Village to the north developed after Adair Air Force Station closed in 1969, and in 1976 became Benton County's newest addition.

We hope you enjoy the following pictures and captions, representing but a small cross-section of the life and times of Benton County residents from the late 1800s to the 1970s.

A PICTORIAL HISTORY

OF BENTON COUNTY

COMMUNITY
PORTRAITS

MANY DIFFERENT HANDS have shaped Benton County history—from the Kalapuya people to the early town platters J.C. Avery and William Dixon, from rural logging crews to Corvallis' Miss Electricity 1885. Some of these images place us face-to-face with the cares and hard work of building lives, fam-

Louis Southworth, an African-American pioneer. Southworth was brought to Benton County as a slave before the Civil War. In the 1850s he purchased his freedom for $1000. He earned this money mainly by teaching violin and playing for dancing schools in the mining camps of Northern California. Southworth's life was full of accomplishments including learning to read and write when such knowledge could be dangerous for a black person. He worked as a blacksmith and was known as a fine horseman. He died in Corvallis on June 23, 1917, less than a month before his 87th birthday. He is buried next to his wife in Crystal Lake Cemetery.

BENTON COUNTY HISTORICAL MUSEUM, HARRIET MOORE COLLECTION, 1994-038.

ilies, and settlements. But look closer, and note the quiet pride that grew naturally out of strenuous daily efforts. Their achievements became part of our legacy.

Here, too, are young faces enjoying childhood and youth in Benton County, and looking optimistically towards its future. The people pictured here were young long ago, though, and we here today share in the fruits of their adult endeavors as well.

The following portraits are but a small cross-section of the people who helped make Benton County what it is today, representing the spirit and determination of these early settlers. Come and sit close by them, and visit with your ancestors in the greater family of our home place.

Above: J.C. Avery, who platted the town of Marysville in 1851. Portrait dates from ca. 1870. In addition to platting the town, Avery had the first store, sawmill, and gristmill, and was one of the incorporators of Corvallis College.

BENTON COUNTY HISTORICAL MUSEUM COLLECTION, 1980-106.0004P.10

Above right: Mary Jane Holmes Shipley Drake, ca. 1924. Mary Jane was the daughter of Robin and Polly Holmes. While her parents, who were slaves, were eventually given their freedom, their children were the object of a custody case between their former master and the Holmeses. Although the court awarded custody to their parents, when Mary Jane married Reuben Shipley in 1857, it is said that a sum of money was demanded of Reuben to be paid in exchange for her freedom.

BENTON COUNTY HISTORICAL MUSEUM, HARRIET MOORE COLLECTION, 1994-038

Right: William F. Dixon. He secured a 617-acre land claim in Benton County in 1846, which shared its southern boundary with J.C. Avery's land claim. When Avery platted the town of Marysville in 1851, Dixon platted an adjacent portion of his claim. These two plats were the first of the town, which was renamed Corvallis in 1853. Dixon is also said to have operated the first ferry on the Willamette River south of Salem.

BENTON COUNTY HISTORICAL MUSEUM, HARRIET MOORE COLLECTION, 1983-019.0083.

Above left: Corvallis businessmen in the early 1880s. Standing left to right: Billy Graham, druggist; Bob Johnson, editor of the *Benton Leader*; Billy Mansfield, printer; Telt Burnett, former sheriff. Seated left to right: Billy Wright, partner in the Brink & Wright Livery Stable; and Samp Henderson, barber.
BENTON COUNTY HISTORICAL MUSEUM, ART LOWE COLLECTION, 1996-100.0058.

Above: Robert James Edwards, downtown Corvallis in 1937.
PHOTO SUBMITTED BY AMY EDWARDS WEIDEMAN, GT 30.

Left: Summit residents "Dutch" and "Irish" McCormick in about 1908—a.k.a. Keith and Kenneth McCormick.
BENTON COUNTY HISTORICAL MUSEUM, MAURICE HUNT COLLECTION, 1997-104.0005.

Above: Members of the Crees family celebrating Christmas in their parlor in the 1890s.

Left: Pleasure Acres circa 1930. Photo collage featuring horse trainer Art Goldblatt and world-famous jockey Earle Sande. Built in the early 1900s, Pleasure Acres had a one-eighth mile indoor track, a clubhouse with elevated stewards' stand, and a perfectly groomed half-mile equestrian racetrack. Currently, Pleasure Acres is located some distance from the road, on the west side of Highway 99W just north of the Corvallis city limits. Originally, Pleasure Acres was located farther to the north on the current site of Hewlett Packard. Upon purchase of the property by Hewlett Packard in the 1970s, the buildings were moved.

Facing page: Corvallis' Miss Electricity, Lulu Maude Miller, ca. 1885.

Above and below: Philomath women, front and back. Photographed by E.V.S. Woodruff ca. 1895. Women are identified left to right as: Nora Hawkins, Belle Ranney, Lillian Ranney, and Ora Henkle.

BENTON COUNTY HISTORICAL MUSEUM, BELLE RANNEY COLLECTION, 1980-106.0001PA AND 1980-106.0001PB.

Above: Logging crew on Ritner Creek, ca. 1900. While Ritner Creek is located in Polk County, this crew is composed of numerous Benton County residents.

BENTON COUNTY HISTORICAL MUSEUM, JAMES McMURTRY COLLECTION, 1994-008.0528.

Right: Christmas Day 1905 wedding portrait of Victor and Lavina "Vina" Wood Moses. Vina Moses was an activist helping those in need in Benton County for over 50 years beginning in 1915. In 1917, she established the Community Welfare Center in the basement of her home. This center still operates today in a different location as the Vina Moses Center.

BENTON COUNTY HISTORICAL MUSEUM, VICTOR AND VINA MOSES COLLECTION, 1980-085.0048P.

She smiled on her Wedding Day.

Above: Bellfountain Cornet Band in 1900. This photograph was taken by W.S. Gardner just before the Old Timers' Picnic.

BENTON COUNTY HISTORICAL MUSEUM, HARRIET MOORE COLLECTION, 1994-038.

Above: Corvallis "Ladies Band", organized and directed by Victor P. Moses from 1894-1900. Victor Moses went on to serve as Benton County Clerk, County Judge, and Corvallis Postmaster. (S.E. TRASK PHOTOGRAPH)

BENTON COUNTY HISTORICAL MUSEUM, HARRIET MOORE COLLECTION, 1983-019.0098.

Below: The Sheriffs of Benton County in 1928. From left to right (with dates served as sheriff noted): Dave Osborn (1892-1896); Peter Rickard (1896-1900); Telt Burnett (1900-1908); Bill Gellatly (1908-1920); and Emery Newton (1925-1936). (HOWELLS PHOTOGRAPH)

BENTON COUNTY HISTORICAL MUSEUM, HARRIET MOORE COLLECTION, 1985-061.0043.

Above: Benton County hunting party, Beaver Creek vicinity.
BENTON COUNTY HISTORICAL MUSEUM, DARRELL EBBERT COLLECTION, 1999-018.0020.

Below: Draft horses in front of the former Hotel Corvallis at the corner of Second Street and Monroe Avenue in Corvallis. The photograph was taken in the first decade of the 20th century. The hotel was remodeled in 1911 and named The Julian Hotel. (GARDNER PHOTOGRAPH)
BENTON COUNTY HISTORICAL MUSEUM, HARRIET MOORE COLLECTION, 1982-004.0113P.

Above: Meeting of the Women's Christian Temperance Union, Benton County, 1910. The W.C.T.U. was very active in Corvallis. According to a 1904 history about the group in Oregon, it was the "moral force" of these women that caused the number of saloons in Corvallis to decrease. The Corvallis headquarters, built in 1884 on Second Street, was the first W.C.T.U. building constructed on the West Coast.

BENTON COUNTY HISTORICAL MUSEUM, DON BRYANS COLLECTION, 1993-049.0027.

Below: Kings Valley tea party, 1913. Florence Graham and Ethel Graham Raw.

PHOTO SUBMITTED BY LOU RAW BAXTER, GT 2.

Above: 1915 Corvallis High School yearbook staff after finishing the last page of the yearbook.
BENTON COUNTY HISTORICAL MUSEUM, HARRIET MOORE COLLECTION, 1982-004.

Below: The Stovall family standing in front of their garden corn crop on their homestead land in King's Valley ca. 1930. Identified from left to right are Frank, Edith May, Francis, little Edith, and George Stovall.
PHOTO SUBMITTED BY GEORGE STOVALL, GT 29.

Above: Corvallis Boy Scout Troop 1 in old troop room in the First Congregational Church located at Eight Street and Madison Avenue. The photograph was taken in December of 1933 for a troop Christmas card.

BENTON COUNTY HISTORICAL MUSEUM, CARL MERRYMAN COLLECTION, 1986-031.

Above: Unidentified Philomath residents at the dinner table after a large meal...possibly Thanksgiving.

Right: The Bellfountain Bells, State Basketball champs, 1937. No Class B high school had ever gone beyond the semi-finals in state tournament play until the Bells beat Portland's Lincoln High School for the state championship in a 35-21 victory. Even more remarkable was the fact that the Bells were an eight-man team from a student body of 28. Upper row left to right: Coach Burton C. Lemmon; K. Stanley Buckingham; Harrison Wallace; Richard "Bunny" Kessler; Frank Buckingham; Clifford Larkin; and Norman Humphrey. Front row: Lynn Hinton and Johnny Key. Bellfountain High School closed in 1938.

A PICTORIAL HISTORY
OF BENTON COUNTY

COMMUNITY
VIEWS

WHEN J.C. AVERY selected a land claim, which encompassed the confluence of the Marys and Willamette rivers late in 1845, he probably already realized the potential of that location for future commercial developments. After constructing a log cabin on the north bank of the Marys River, he reportedly fenced off a 12-acre parcel of land known as the "little field." In the winter of 1847-1848, he staked off a few town lots in this field located at what today would be the southern extremity of Second Street. Town development waited, however, for shortly thereafter gold was discovered in California and most able-bodied men, including Avery, left for the gold fields. When Avery returned from a second California trip in 1849, he brought goods to open a store. The site of this first store was in Avery's granary near his cabin. In 1850, the post office of Avery was established, with J.C. Avery as postmaster. That same year, he erected a larger store on the corner of what is presently Second and Washington, and in the latter part of that year began to lay out the town of Marysville, the plat of which was filed in 1851. In 1853, the town's name was changed to Corvallis, a

name supposedly made up by Avery by compounding Latin words meaning "Heart of the Valley." This change was made to prevent confusion with Marysville, California.

Many of Benton County's earliest communities were located on the first trails and roads through the area such as the Territorial Road, the major north-south route through western Oregon on the west side of the Willamette River. In north Benton County, the Tampico post office, first known as Soap

Above: Hoskins, Oregon. A covered bridge can be seen in the foreground. The building in the center of the photograph with the two-story porch is the store. Headquarters for the Valley and Siletz Railroad Company, the little community prospered until the early 1950s, when the railroad ceased operations. The tracks were removed, and today little remains of Hoskins.

BENTON COUNTY HISTORICAL MUSEUM, HARRIET MOORE COLLECTION, 1994-038.

Creek, was established in 1854; an eight-block plat for Tampico townsite was filed in 1857. The town, located on the Territorial Road, had a number of businesses, including the Arcade saloon, a school, a boarding house, and a blacksmith shop. It also had a reputation for being a rather lively place with gambling, especially horse racing, a popular activity. A twelve-verse song of the era addresses a rivalry that existed between Corvallis and Tampico, a rivalry ending abruptly in 1860. Greenberry Smith, a money lender who managed to acquire all of the property in the town, annulled the town plat and vacated it.

At the site of what is presently known as Winkle Buttes, on Highway 99W, the post office of Jennyopolis was established in 1852. Like Tampico, Jennyopolis was situated on the Territorial Road. In addition to the post office, Jennyopolis had a store and saloon. At the time the post office was established, the "town" was situated in the area between the two buttes; the route changed shortly thereafter to an alignment similar to that of the present Highway 99W. At that time, the store and post office are believed to have been moved to the west side of the smaller butte. The post office was closed in 1857, but the store continued to serve travelers.

In south Benton County, just north of the present town of Monroe, the Starr's Point post office was established in 1852 with Samuel F. Starr appointed the first postmaster. That same year, Roland Hinton replaced Starr as postmaster. Mr. Hinton erected a large frame house, which also served as a tavern and a stage stop for travelers on the Territorial Road. Nearby, George Starr and Silas Belknap oversaw a store. Although the stage stop and tavern continued to operate in the 1860s, Starr's Point was eclipsed by the platting of the town of Monroe in 1857.

Many late 19th century and early 20th century communities were established as post offices in cross-road locations. These include Alpine (post office 1912); Bellfountain, originally known as Dusty (post office 1895); Rickard (post office 1877-1881); Bruce (post office 1900); Fern (post office 1899); Inavale (post office 1896-1905); and Brown (post office 1902). Some of these post offices closed in the first decade of the 20th century as a consequence of rural free delivery. Alpine and Bellfountain developed into regional service centers in the early 1900s.

Gristmills spurred the establishment of several early Benton County communities. Since farmers brought their grain to the mills to be ground, these locations often became the nucleus for regional trading centers. Kings Valley is named for early settlers Nahum and Serepta Norton King and their extended family, who settled the area from the Luckiamute River south to the Marys River. A gristmill was established on the Luckiamute River by Rowland Chambers, son-in-law of Nahum King, in the early 1850s; the post office known as Kings Valley was established in 1855 with Rowland Chambers, first postmaster. In 1868, G.C. Nelson opened a store, and by 1880 the community of Kings Valley consisted of three stores, a saloon, a grocery, a blacksmith shop, and a hotel.

William Matzger operated a sawmill just west of the present town of Philomath, adding a gristmill in 1854. The gristmill was known as the Matzger and Hartless Mill, and later as the Marys River Flouring Mills. A race dug from the Marys River supplied the water power to operate the mill. The small community that sprang up around the mill included a school, a tannery, a Methodist Church, and residences. In the latter part of the 19th century, Jacob Felger operated the mill, but Philomath–established in the mid-1860s–eclipsed the early community.

In the early 1850s, Joseph White operated a sawmill on the Long Tom River. A gristmill succeeded the sawmill in that location, and the store and post office, previously located at Starr's Point to the north, moved to the gristmill location in 1854. In 1857, the town of Monroe was platted in this location, although the name of the post office was not changed to Monroe until 1874.

A gristmill was established in the Alsea Valley in 1873. A settlement, however, had already existed for a number of years in the valley, with the name Alseya Settlement appearing on the Surveyor General's map in 1855. The post office of Alsea was not established until 1871, and it was not until 1908 that the town of Alsea was platted. The town developed into a regional trade center in the early 20th century. The Lobster post office in Lobster Valley was established in 1883 and closed in 1896.

Steamboat traffic on the Willamette River gave rise to a number of steamboat landings. In Benton County, from north to south, were: Spring Hill, Rainwater's Landing, Bower's Rocks, Eckland's Landing, Irish Boy's Landing, Dow's Landing, and Finley's Landing. Booneville, located approximately five miles south of Corvallis, was platted as a townsite in 1853. The townsite, which stretched for nine blocks, was located on the main channel of the Willamette River and was considered the best landing between Corvallis and Lancaster (near Harrisburg). A warehouse located there served as a receiving and shipping point for wheat grown in the region. The town also had a blacksmith shop and store.

The construction of rail lines through Benton County generated a number of rural communities ranging from small towns to railroad crossings, where farm products could be delivered for shipment. Among the communities established as a result of the completion of the Western Oregon Railway line from Portland to Corvallis were the communities of Wells, Peavy, and Lewisburg.

The completion of the Oregon Pacific Railroad late in 1884 led to the establishment of the communities of Wren, Harris (called Elam when the post office was established in 1918), Blodgett, and Summit. The Wren post office was established in 1887 and is named for George P. Wrenn, an early settler in the area who later moved to Corvallis. Wrenn died in 1882 while fighting a grain warehouse fire in Corvallis. The town of Wren grew to include a general store, boarding house, train depot, sawmill, and planing mill. At the turn of the 20th century, Harris had a large steam-powered sawmill as well as a train depot, store, church, and school. In 1888 the post office of Emerick was established; that same year the name was changed to Blodgett. Summit was platted in 1885 by William Post. Its name is derived from its location as the highest point of the rail line. Around 1890, a general store was erected and, in 1898, the Summit post office was established. Summit was the maintenance headquarters for the O & P, and eventually grew to include several stores, a railroad depot, and a boarding house, as well as a church, school, and grange hall.

Smaller stops that developed along the route included Flynn, near the current junction of Highways 34 and 20 and the terminus of a log flume; Noon Siding, a siding for the W.C. Noon Logging Company; Conger; Russell; Alder (Hipp post office 1922); Marval; and Devitt. Devitt was a mill town that supported a cluster of houses, a general store, and a school for employees of the Devitt Brothers Sawmill there. A post office was established in 1919 and closed in 1933. The mill burned in the 1930s and was never rebuilt. When the rail line was extended to Albany in 1887, stops included Granger (post office 1888) and North Albany.

In 1911-1912, the rail line was extended south from Corvallis to Monroe. Stops along this route included Avery, Dry Creek, Schrock, Greenberry, Buchanan, Barclay, and Burnett. Baily Junction and Alpine Junction were located on spur lines which served large mills located at Glenbrook and Dawson. Glenbrook's post office predated the rail line, however, having been established in 1898.

Two Benton County communities have military associations. Fort Hoskins was established in 1856 for the purpose of guarding the central entrance to the newly formed Siletz Indian Reservation. The post operated with regular Army troops until the outbreak of the Civil War, during which volunteers were employed. The fort was decommissioned in 1865 and the property was acquired by the Frantz family. While a number of sawmills had operated in this area prior to the 1870s, the Frantz brothers established the Kings Valley Saw and Planing Mill, and store, at this site. The Hoskins post office was established in 1891, and in 1912 Hoskins became the headquarters of the Valley and Siletz

Railroad, with a company-owned store, bunkhouse, shop, and roundhouse. The Valley and Siletz Railroad, built along the Luckiamute River, was completed from Independence to Valsetz in 1917, primarily to transport logs and lumber from sawmills. The line also carried passengers, farm produce, and mail. As a result, the community of Hoskins grew to include a bank and hotel.

The roots of Adair Village are traced to the establishment of Camp Adair, a World War II military cantonment dating from 1942. In order to construct this facility, families were uprooted,

housing units, a gymnasium, church, officers and enlisted men's clubs, and a base exchange. After 12 years of operation the installation was closed and declared surplus by the federal government. In 1972, Benton County acquired 75 acres for use as a park, and the following year the housing units were acquired by a private developer for sale. Adair Village was incorporated in 1976.

One Benton County community was established by a religious group. In 1853, the arrival of the Connor-Kenoyer missionary party contributed to a strong United Brethren presence in central

Above: Kings Valley looking north from town to the covered bridge over the Luckiamute River. Known as Kings Valley as early as 1854, the area was settled by Nahum and Serepta King and their children, who came in the spring of 1846.
HORNER MUSEUM, 1981-060-4.

cemeteries were relocated, and the small community of Wells was erased. Camp Adair was the home base for four army units: the 91st, the 96th, the 70th, and the 104th. Here these units trained for overseas duty. At one point during the war, Camp Adair was the second-largest "city" in Oregon. A portion of the camp was also used for Italian and German prisoners of war.

At war's end, increased enrollment of Oregon State College created a demand for housing. The college remodeled some of the Adair hospital buildings for housing, and the locality was renamed Adair Village—with its own post office established in 1947. In 1957, the federal government began planning for the Adair Air Force Station on this property. The purpose of this installation was to provide automatic surveillance as part of an early warning system to guard against ballistic missile attacks. In addition to the SAGE blockhouse, the Air Force station had approximately 150

Benton County. In 1865, the United Brethren Church acquired the Henderson donation land claim upon which they founded Philomath College and platted the town of Philomath. The town prospered to become a dominant regional trading center eclipsing the small settlements centered around Matzger's Mill and Mount Union.

Homesteaders continued to come to Benton County in the late 19th and early 20th centuries. Among the areas settled was the northwest flank of Marys Peak. A road, known as the Old Ridge or Old Peak Road, from Philomath to Elk City, passed through the Harrison Davidson Claim. Mrs. Davidson requested a post office and the post office of Peak was established in 1899 in her living room. This post office operated until 1917. A store and school were also established in this location, but today there is no trace of the community except for a cemetery.

Left: Inside Kings Valley store. Florence Graham, "Jake" Chambers, and Ethel Graham Raw. "Jake" Chambers is the son of Rowland Chambers, son-in-law of Nahum and Serepta King.

PHOTO SUBMITTED BY LOU RAW BAXTER, GT 3.

Below: Log boom and mill, Hoskins, Oregon, around 1908. Between 1900 and 1940, the timber industry was the most important economic force in the Kings Valley region.

BENTON COUNTY HISTORICAL MUSEUM, BERNICE SMITH COLLECTION. 1991-090.0073.

Above: Kings Valley, Oregon, in 1914. Identified from left to right are Ethel Graham Raw, Florence Graham, and Abbie Graham Freeman.

Above: Building the Summit-Blodgett Highway, early 20th century. PHOTO COURTESY OF MARLENE McDONALD

Below: View of Summit, early 20th century. Railroad, depot, and store pictured in the foreground. MAURICE BULLARD COLLECTION, 1984-099.0011

Above: First Wren Store, early 1900s.

PHOTO COURTESY OF GEORGE AND RITA JOHNSON. WREN 3.

Below: View of Blodgett, early 20th century.

BENTON COUNTY HISTORICAL MUSEUM, WILLARD DAVIS COLLECTION 2000-002-0002

Above: Aerial view of Philomath looking west to Marys Peak. The photograph was probably taken from the upper floors of the Philomath College Building. Houses along Tenth Street are in the foreground, and the Philomath Public School, built in 1900, can be seen in the distance.

Facing page, top: Alpine, Oregon in 1912. Alpine experienced a period of growth in the early 20th Century. It boasted several buildings, including a hotel and opera house. Disastrous fires in 1918 and 1924 virtually leveled the town. After the second fire, Alpine never fully recovered.

Facing page, bottom: Town of Alsea, Oregon (before 1909). Large building on right was the general store of Chandler and Houser. The name "Alseya Settlement" first appears on the Surveyor General's Map of 1855. However, the first post office was established in 1871. The name "Alsea" is probably derived from the name of the Native Americans who lived at the mouth of the river.

n St. Philomath, Ore.

Main Street Philomath in the early 20th century, looking west near the intersection of Main and Thirteenth streets. Philomath was established in 1865 when land was purchased and lots were sold by the United Brethren Church to finance the building of Philomath College. The name Philomath is from the Greek; it means "a lover of learning" or scholar.

BENTON COUNTY HISTORICAL MUSEUM, HARRIET MOORE COLLECTION, 1994-038.

Above: Third Street in Corvallis looking south from the intersection of Monroe Avenue in 1926. The Crees Building, presently housing the Book Bin on the main floor, is seen under construction.

BENTON COUNTY HISTORICAL MUSEUM, EDNA WIESE COLLECTION, 1990-068.1307.

Below: Second Street in Corvallis in 1873, looking north from the intersection of Second Street and Jefferson Avenue.

BENTON COUNTY HISTORICAL MUSEUM PRINT FROM RALPH PARKHURST NEGATIVE, 1998-001.0026.

Above: Aerial view of Corvallis looking to the northwest. This photograph was taken sometime between 1903 and 1909. In the foreground is Second Street near the Jefferson Avenue intersection.

BENTON COUNTY HISTORICAL MUSEUM, ANDREW GELLATLY COLLECTION, 1984-038.0008

Above: Looking west on Monroe Avenue between Third and Fourth streets in the late 1920s. The Elks Building was located on the southeast corner of Fourth Street and Monroe Avenue. The truck is from the Corvallis Laundry.
BENTON COUNTY HISTORICAL MUSEUM, MR. AND MRS. HAROLD LEHNERT COLLECTION, 1981-002.0019P.

Left: Second Street in Corvallis in 1929, looking north from just south of the Madison Avenue intersection. Second Street was still a hub of activity although the business district had expanded to Third Street. (PHOTOGRAPH BY HOWELLS)
BENTON COUNTY HISTORICAL MUSEUM, EDNA WIESE COLLECTION, 1990-068.1397.

Below: Looking to the southwest from the water tower once located near the corner of Second Street and Adams Avenue in Corvallis. A rare view of Corvallis' first railroad depot is in the upper left of the photograph, and the J.C. Avery Building, presently Robnett's Hardware and the oldest commercial building in Corvallis, is located in the right foreground. HORNER MUSEUM COLLECTION, 10140-6.

Above: Aerial view of Corvallis in 1923. Note the Oregon Electric train station on the east side of the Van Buren Street Bridge. (BALL STUDIO PHOTOGRAPH) PHOTO SUBMITTED BY ROBERT LOWRY, GT 33.

Below: Boardwalk from town to campus early 1890s. Lower campus extended to present-day Ninth Street. The boardwalk was located between Madison and Jefferson avenues. Note the baseball game being played. BENTON COUNTY HISTORICAL MUSEUM, EDNA WIESE COLLECTION, 1990-068.1302.

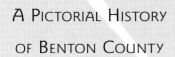

A Pictorial History
of Benton County

Buildings
and Businesses

SECOND STREET, between Monroe and Adams, was the heart of the first commercial district in 19th century Corvallis. Wooden one- and two-story, gabled, brick, and false-fronted buildings lined the wide dirt thoroughfare where livery stables, saloons, blacksmith shops, general stores, drug stores, butcher shops, and hotels hung out their signs. With the arrival of the railroad late in 1879, a period of optimism fueled further construction. Two-story brick buildings with facades embellished by cast iron and pressed metal architectural ornaments imparted a more permanent character to the business district.

A new county courthouse was a consequence of the euphoria generated by the completion of a second rail line in 1885. The imposing Benton County Courthouse, completed in 1888, was designed by Portland architect Delos D. Neer, who described the building as Italianate with a military influence. At present, it is the oldest courthouse in Oregon still used for its original purpose.

In the early 20th century, the traditional business district expanded to Third Street, a move launched by the relocation of the Nolan Store to the newly constructed Harding Building on the northwest corner of Third and Madison in 1910. At the same time, surviving 19th century wood buildings on Second Street were demolished and replaced by buildings with gleaming facades of colored pressed brick and concrete punctuated by large expanses of plate glass windows. Housed in these buildings were businesses not dreamed of in the previous century—such as automobile garages, gas stations, department stores and movie theaters. The Whiteside Brothers, Sam and George, operated a number of theaters in Corvallis including the Palace, the Crystal, and the Majestic. In 1922, anxious to have their own building, they erected the Whiteside Theater on Madison Avenue, a structure in the tradition of the grand movie palaces of the 1920s.

By the late 1920s, commerce had reached Fourth Street. With the exception of two notable buildings, however, construction came almost to a standstill in Corvallis during the early years of the Great Depression. In 1931, both the Corvallis Public Library and the present Corvallis Post Office were completed. The library was designed by internationally-renowned 20th century architect Pietro Belluschi.

In Benton County's rural communities in the 19th century, most of the commercial buildings were wood frame. Each community had at least one mercantile store, often with a two-story prominence. In Philomath, there were the J.E. Henkle & Co. general store and the Moses Brothers General Merchandise store. Only Monroe, Alsea, and Philomath saw the addition of masonry and concrete buildings in the early 20th century, with bank buildings among the first of these more permanent buildings to be constructed in each community. In Monroe, Adam Wilhelm replaced his earlier general store with a large department store housed in a brick building on Main Street.

Sawmills and gristmills were the earliest industrial ventures, with waterpower initially used to operate machinery. Often it was the location of a gristmill that prompted the establishment of a town since farmers would often combine a trip to the mill with trading at local businesses. Early gristmills were located in Kings Valley, Monroe, Corvallis, and near Inavale and Alsea. In the later part of the 19th century, several flour mills were quite successful, their product marketed far wider than Benton County. These included the Wilhelm Mill in Monroe, and the Fischer Mill and Benton County Flouring Mills in Corvallis. In Corvallis, the riverfront was a location for 19th century industrial developments, including warehouses for the storage of grain to be shipped by river. Similar warehouses could be found along the river in rural areas of the county at long-forgotten steamboat landings such as Liverpool and Booneville.

Sawmills were located in many rural and non-rural county areas, sometimes moving with the supply and demand for lumber locally. Water- and steam-powered sawmills were operating in the early 1850s in some locations. Other pioneer-era industries included fanning mills, carding mills, tanneries, and sash and door factories. In the early 20th century, rise of the timber industry in Oregon spawned large mills in communities such as Hoskins, Dawson, Glenbrook, Philomath, and Corvallis.

COMMERCE

Right: Occidental Lumber Company sawmill in the Beaver Creek area ca. 1910. Note the flume leading to an overshot water wheel, which provided the power to operate the mill.
BENTON COUNTY HISTORICAL MUSEUM, CORVALLIS PUBLIC LIBRARY COLLECTION, 1985-032.0025AM.

Above: The Corvallis Carriage and Wagon Co., organized in 1891. In 1892, the company erected this building on the Oregon and Pacific Railroad tracks on the blocks between Eleventh and Thirteenth streets. Many local people bought stock in the company. However, Western oak was very different from Eastern oak. Western oak cracked and checked even after it was made into vehicles. Furthermore, salespeople already had long-term contracts with eastern firms and could not purchase from the local company. What had appeared to be a promising enterprise was a complete failure. In 1896, the carriage factory closed.
BENTON COUNTY HISTORICAL MUSEUM, HARRIET MOORE COLLECTION, 1994-038.

The Corvallis Lumber Company, located on the flat on the north side of the confluence of the Willamette and Marys rivers. This mill was established in 1909 as the McCready Brothers Sawmill. Photograph taken ca. 1940.
PHOTO SUBMITTED BY BARBARA HAYS, GT 32.

The Horning Carding Mill, located just to the northwest of the Western Avenue and 35th Street intersection. A flume and overshot water wheel, with water provided by Oak Creek, powered the carding mill. An early Benton County settler, R.C. Motley, recalled that, "In the evenings, the boys were put to work picking the wool which later was taken to a little carding mill on Oak Creek." This mill was destroyed by fire in 1869 but was rebuilt.
BENTON COUNTY HISTORICAL MUSEUM, HARRIET MOORE COLLECTION, 1985-061.0046.

The Benton County Flouring Mills was perhaps the largest of the grain-related businesses located along First Street on the Willamette River in Corvallis. Beginning in the early 1850s, when steamboats first tied up at Corvallis' wharves, the bank was lined with warehouses and industrial buildings. This mill was erected in 1890 and was located between Monroe and Jackson avenues. Much of the flour produced at this mill went to foreign markets.
BENTON COUNTY HISTORICAL MUSEUM, HARRIET MOORE COLLECTION, 1994-038.

Above: Moses Bros. Department Store, 1904. This business, located on the south-west corner of Main and Thirteenth streets in Philomath, was a hub of activity in Philomath for forty-seven years. The wagon was used for home delivery.
BENTON COUNTY HISTORICAL MUSEUM, VICTOR AND VINA MOSES COLLECTION, 1980-085.0053P.

Top: The first Wilhelm store in Monroe, during the late 19th century.
PHOTO SUBMITTED BY VERNETTA McCALLUM, GT 21.

Middle: In 1885 the Corvallis Water Co. was organized to provide a gravity flow water system. In 1888 the company built this water tower just west of the corner of First and Adams. The City of Corvallis purchased the Corvallis Water Co. in 1892.
BENTON COUNTY HISTORICAL MUSEUM, HARRIET MOORE COLLECTION, 1994-038.

Bottom: Emanuel Meier and friends in front of car garage on Second Street in Corvallis, 1911. Emanuel is the center person between the two cars, one of which he built. Mr. Meier was a partner in Riley and Meier Dodge car dealership during the 1920s. The garage was on Second Street, which is now where the Old World Center is located.
PHOTO SUBMITTED BY SHELDON MEIER, GT 24.

Above: Looking north, view of Second Street between Jefferson and Adams, circa 1905.

PHOTO SUBMITTED BY IRENE CHILDEARS, GT 7.

Below: The Interior of Blackledge Furniture in Corvallis, circa 1903.

PHOTO SUBMITTED BY ROBERT BLACKLEDGE, GT 4.

Above: The inside of Lesh's Luscious Loafs, a bakery and candy store located on Second Street, ca. 1915-1920. Pictured is Eleanor Lesh. PHOTO SUBMITTED BY KATHRYN SCHULTZ, GT 28.

Left: The J.H. Harris Dry Goods Store, 1889. This business was located in the Burnett Building which still exists, although altered, on the southwest corner of Second Street and Madison Avenue in Corvallis. (PERNOT BROS. PHOTOGRAPH)
BENTON COUNTY HISTORICAL MUSEUM, NANCY HARRIS COLLECTION, 1989-134.0003.

Below: City Hotel, ca. 1865. Located on the southwest corner of Second Street and Madison Avenue in Corvallis, the widow's walk atop the hotel provided a view of the river and of arriving and departing steamboats. The hotel was destroyed by fire in 1873. David D. Fagan's *History of Benton County, Oregon*, written in 1885, reports, "Such a wild scene was never witnessed before in Corvallis. Men, women and children escaped from the burning pile and rushed out into a cold rain storm with nothing on but their sleeping garments...Several persons saved their lives by slipping down a lamp post." John Murray, the visiting father-in-law of the proprietor, died in the fire.
BENTON COUNTY HISTORICAL MUSEUM, FRANK GROVES COLLECTION, 1980-088.0078P.

Facing page, top: Inside Corl's Bookstore, Corvallis, in the early 1920s. Corl's Bookstore closed in 1990 after three generations of Corl family ownership.
PHOTO SUBMITTED BY ROB CORL, GT 9.

Facing page, bottom: Hotel Corvallis, located on the southeast corner of Second Street and Monroe Avenue, was built in 1893. An extensive remodeling in 1910-1911 added a story, removed the corner tower, and removed and replaced the walls. The revamped hotel was renamed the Julian Hotel for owner Julian McFadden. Presently listed on the National Register of Historic Places, the Julian looks much as it did in 1911.
BENTON COUNTY HISTORICAL MUSEUM, FLOSSIE OVERMAN COLLECTION, 1986-059.0132V.

Above: Corvallis Creamery Co., ca. 1915. The Corvallis Creamery was established in 1897 at a time when dairying took on greater importance regionally. This building was erected in the early years of the 20th century and was located on First Street just south of Madison Avenue. In 1931, the Corvallis Creamery became Medo-land Creamery Co. Note the railroad, which served the businesses along First Street.

BENTON COUNTY HISTORICAL MUSEUM, ART LOWE COLLECTION, 1996-100.0002.

Facing page, top: The front of Montgomery Ward store on Second and Jefferson in downtown Corvallis, around 1928.

PHOTO SUBMITTED BY VIRGINIA C. WEIR, GT 31.

Facing page, middle: The Corvallis Steam Laundry located on the east side of Second Street between Jackson and Van Buren, in the early 1900s. Steam laundries were very popular in the 1920s because, until the arrival of the washing machine, they reduced the Monday washing for middle-class women.

PHOTO SUBMITTED BY THE GERDING FAMILY, GT 15.

Facing page, bottom: The Benton County National Bank Building, ca. 1910. Located on the northeast corner of Second Street and Madison Avenue in Corvallis, this Romanesque style bank building was built in 1907, and is currently listed on the National Register of Historic Places. Turkish baths and a barbershop were located in the basement.

BENTON COUNTY HISTORICAL MUSEUM, HAROLD LEHNERT COLLECTION, 1981-002.0023P.

Above: Built in 1922, the Ball Building was located at the northwest corner of Third Street and Jefferson Avenue in Corvallis. Ball Studio was located on the ground floor and apartments were upstairs. When the building burned in 1939, studio records dating back to 1912 were destroyed. Studio films for the Oregon State College yearbook of 1939 were also destroyed. The *Corvallis Gazette-Times* reported that this was particularly unfortunate, since this was the first time the yearbook had been edited by a woman. Students were anxious to see if the work equaled or excelled the yearbooks previously published by men.
BENTON COUNTY HISTORICAL MUSEUM, ART LOWE COLLECTION, 1996-100.0025.

Left: Nolan's Department Store in 1934. Located in the 1910 Harding Building, which still stands on the northwest corner of Third Street and Madison Avenue in Corvallis, Nolan's was the first major retailer to move from Second Street to Third Street. At that time, Nolan's advertised that "it paid to walk a little farther." The Nolan's corner eventually became the center of retail trade in Corvallis. At the time of construction, the stretch of 170 feet of plate glass display windows was considered a magnificent feature of the building. (HOWELLS PHOTOGRAPH)
BENTON COUNTY HISTORICAL MUSEUM, EDNA WIESE COLLECTION, 1990-068.1333.

Below: Veterinarian Dr. J.E. Rohner in front of his Corvallis office on the corner of Fourth and Harrison, ca. 1930.
PHOTO SUBMITTED BY MARLENE FURMAN, GT 14.

Public Buildings

Right: Drawing of the first Benton County Courthouse from an 1859 Kuchel and Dresel lithograph. This courthouse, built in 1855, was located on the same block as the current courthouse in Corvallis.

BENTON COUNTY HISTORICAL MUSEUM, HARLAND PRATT COLLECTION, 1999-060.0044.

Below: Benton County Courthouse in the early 20th century prior to being painted white in 1913. The courthouse was listed on the National Register of Historic Places in 1977, and is the oldest courthouse still used for its original purpose in the State of Oregon. The architect, Delos D. Neer, described the style of the courthouse as Italianate with a military influence.

BENTON COUNTY HISTORICAL MUSEUM, CORVALLIS PUBLIC LIBRARY COLLECTION, 1985-032.0025X.

Above: Benton County Jail, 1929. This jail was located on the north side of the courthouse and fronted west onto Fifth Street. Built in 1929, the jail was demolished when the present jail was constructed.

BENTON COUNTY HISTORICAL MUSEUM, BETTY HICKMAN COLLECTION, 1988-002.0007.

Left: Corvallis City Hall, built in 1892, was located on the southeast corner of Fourth Street and Madison Avenue. The fire companies were originally housed on the lower level until a fire department was built on the south side of the building. The City Hall building and fire department were demolished in the 1950s to make way for the Lipman's Building, which was completed in 1959.

BENTON COUNTY HISTORICAL MUSEUM, CORVALLIS PUBLIC LIBRARY COLLECTION, 1985-032.0025BJ.

Below: Lobby of the Corvallis Post Office, 1932. This photograph was taken shortly after the completion of the Post Office Building, which is still in use at the southeast corner of Second Street and Jefferson Avenue in Corvallis. The contractor for the post office, J. Thomsen, was also the contractor for the original section of the Corvallis Public Library.

BENTON COUNTY HISTORICAL MUSEUM, ERNEST AND LEE RUDISELL COLLECTION, 1992-025.0009BG.

SCHOOLS

SCHOOLHOUSES WERE AMONG the first buildings erected once the settlers took care of the more pressing needs of food and shelter. The rural school site, which was often one acre, contained the schoolhouse, a wood shed, two outhouses, perhaps a horse shed, and sometimes play equipment. The schoolhouse was usually a rectangular, front-gabled building with one room. The outsides of schoolhouses ranged from crude, unpainted board, to exteriors finished with painted trim elements. Many of the first schools were of log construction, like the schoolhouse erected in 1848 on what is currently the northeast corner of Second and Jackson in Corvallis and the Gingles Schoolhouse, located in the North Albany area.

Many log schoolhouses were replaced in the early 1850s, including the schoolhouse in Corvallis, because of the availability of sawn lumber. Emma Horning Groves, who attended the Corvallis school in the 1850s, recalled, "The old schoolhouse where I went to school was on the east side of Fifth Street, across from the College. We took our lunch and would spend the noon hour playing in the college while it was being built." (The Corvallis College building was under construction on the west side of Fifth Street, between Monroe and Madison, in 1859.)

Most students walked, while some rode horses to the district schoolhouse—often a mile or more away but rarely farther than five miles from home. Many schools were closed in the worst winter months because of deep mud and heavy rains. In the summer, farm work closed the schools, leaving several months in the fall and spring for classes.

Schoolhouses were also the social hubs of communities, because the schools sponsored many community events. Popular amusements included box socials, pie socials, and ice cream socials. Christmas, May Day and graduation were among the most important days for school celebrations.

Prior to the establishment of school districts in 1852, anyone could teach school. Even when districts were established, the county superintendent examined prospective teachers' qualifications, but no college training was required. Since salaries were low, trained teachers, especially men, preferred to teach in town or at a college and, therefore, the rural school became the domain of unmarried women. By 1874, teachers were required to pass standardized tests and those who wanted to upgrade their teaching certificates had to attend normal school.

In 1897, rural schools began to be graded, with the eighth grade examination required. Previously, students had learned at their own pace. A course of study prescribing what a student should learn each year was instituted, with children passing from grade to grade instead of reader to reader. If students passed the eighth grade exam with a grade of ninety percent or better, they could be admitted to college. For most, however, eighth grade was the end of school, especially in rural areas where high schools were unavailable.

Corvallis was the first district to have multiple-room schools in Benton County. In 1864, the district was divided along Madison Street. Two new schools were built: the North District School (1866) and the South District School (1867). The North District School was located on Fifth and Harrison streets and the South District School was located on the southwest corner of Fifth and "B" streets. In 1887, the South School burned. The Corvallis School District purchased the land upon which a former Episcopal School was located, tore down the school building and built a new grade school in the block bounded by Monroe and Madison streets and Seventh and Eighth streets in 1889. This two-story, wood-frame building with eight large classrooms was known as Central School.

In Philomath, a two-room school was completed in 1881. In the more rural communities, multiple-room schools were not built until after the turn of the 20th century, the consequence of increased population and/or consolidation. Multiple room schools, some in two story buildings, were erected in the following districts: Alsea; Monroe; Summit; Blodgett; Bellfountain; Fir Grove; Fairplay; Kings Valley; Mountain View; North Albany; Oak Grove; Irish Bend, and Lincoln, which was originally a rural school district south of Corvallis.

In Corvallis, new schools were erected in the early 20th century as the boundaries of the city expanded. New schools included Roosevelt (1912); College Hill School, later known as Harding (1923-1924); and Washington School, currently the Benton Center (1923-1924). Central School was converted to a junior high school until the present Corvallis High School was built in 1935; at that time the old high school, built in 1909-1910, became Corvallis Junior High School. In 1938, a Public Works Administration project enlarged Harding School, adding an auditorium, classrooms, and a basement.

The one-room schoolhouse was still the standard in many rural areas of Benton County until the 1940s, when the State of Oregon decreed that all elementary districts must be part of high school districts. This edict, combined with school buses and an all-weather road network, resulted in consolidation for many school districts. Among the districts with high schools in the early years of the 20th century were Kings Valley, Philomath, Monroe, and Corvallis. Bellfountain added a high school curriculum in 1906, setting aside two classrooms in the 1908 building for the high school. In Alsea, twelve grades were accommodated in a single building.

There were also a number of religious schools established in Benton County at an early date. Among the earliest was Corvallis College, purchased in 1860 by the Methodist Episcopal Church South. In 1865, the United Brethren Church platted the City of Philomath and established Philomath College. In 1889, a division in the United Brethren Church led to the establishment of a second college in Philomath known as the College of Philomath. After college president J.C. Keezel had a fatal fall from the roof of the building being constructed for the college, his wife, Sarah Keezel, became president, a rare position for a woman in the 19th century. The Episcopal congregation built a school and chapel in 1871 variously known as Chapel School, St. Helens, and eventually Good Samaritan. The building was located in what is now Central Park in Corvallis.

Some of the above information was summarized from the book, *When School Bells Rang: Schools of Benton County, Oregon*, by Marlene McDonald.

Top: Auxiliary School, a one-room Benton County school-house, was located on Bellfountain Road on what is now the Finley Wildlife Refuge. In the 1860s, the school terms were three months. Sometimes there were two terms, if weather and farm work permitted. This photograph probably dates to the 1890s.

BENTON COUNTY HISTORICAL MUSEUM, HARRIET MOORE COLLECTION, 1994-038.

Middle: The little Red Schoolhouse, Wren's one room schoolhouse at the intersection of Highway 223 and Cardwell Hill Drive, 1909.

PHOTO COURTESY OF DOROTHY BROWN AND THEODORE GUMP, WREN 1.

Bottom: Alsea Public School with "kiddie wagons" used to transport children "from as far away as five miles." Alsea School District was among the first to consolidate a number of rural districts and the "kiddie wagons," in the years before school buses, were an essential part of the plan. The building featured a painted clock on the tower. The school was built in 1909 and burned in 1930.

BENTON COUNTY HISTORICAL MUSEUM, HAZEL McNEILL RYCRAFT COLLECTION, 1982-081.

Above: Inside a Philomath College classroom, ca. 1910.

Right: Children jumping rope at Ward School in the early 1950s. Ward School was located on Maxfield Creek Road between the communities of Kings Valley and Airlie in Polk County. The teacher was housed in the mobile home behind the schoolhouse until the school closed in 1958.

Above: The Philomath College Building was constructed in 1867 for the United Brethren Church, which established both the town and college of Philomath. This is perhaps the earliest photograph of the building that presently houses the Benton County Historical Museum. The building today has two large wings that were added in the early 20th century.

Above: Alpine school ceremony at Bellfountain Park, June 1901. Pictured, from left to right, are: Merle Howard, Ira Goodman, Ralph Hawley, Frank Williams, Preston Hammer, Ivan Hawley, Earl Hawley, Inez Williams, Pearl Hammer, Golda Howard Ayelsworth Belknap, Cora Hawley, Reta Price, Floy Hawley, and Edith Price.
PHOTO SUBMITTED BY JUDY ANN BUTLER, GT 5.

Below: Located in Central Park, this school building was erected in 1903 to alleviate overcrowding in Central School. In 1909, it was moved to make room for a larger high school building. This school was cut in two for its move to Eighteenth and Polk streets, where it served as a grade school first known as North School and later known as Franklin School.
BENTON COUNTY HISTORICAL MUSEUM, HARRIET MOORE COLLECTION. 1994-038.

Above: Bellfountain Intermediate School, class photo 1915-1918. Identified in the back row, tallest, is Marvin Coon.

PHOTO SUBMITTED BY MARGARET COON, GT 8.

Left: The original Mountain View School at Lewisburg and the school class of 1944-1945. The teacher resided in the top floor and class was held in the lower level. This older building sat to the north of the current school building. At the time the photo was taken, the school was two rooms with four grades in each room.

PHOTO SUBMITTED BY LORRAINE DOUGHERTY, GT 11.

Below: Corvallis High School, ca. 1913. Located on the east block of the two-block area that is now Central Park, Corvallis High School was built in 1909-1910, and was enlarged in 1917. This building housed Corvallis Junior High School after the construction of the present Corvallis High School in 1935. In 1946 the building was destroyed in a spectacular fire.

BENTON COUNTY HISTORICAL MUSEUM,
MARGARET SNYDER JOHNSON ESTATE COLLECTION, 1984-015.0106.

Above: Wells Public and High School was located in what is now E.E. Wilson Wildlife Refuge in northern Benton County. In 1942, the military appeared at the school door and told the teacher that was the last day of school. The town of Wells was "removed" that year for the construction of Camp Adair.
BENTON COUNTY HISTORICAL MUSEUM, VELMA RAWIE COLLECTION, 1983-029.0001.

Below: Central School, built in 1889, was located in what is now Central Park in Corvallis. The school building, which faced east, was located on the west block of the two blocks, which now make up the park. This view illustrates the rear of the building and the play shed erected in the early 20th century. The school building was dismantled in 1935.
BENTON COUNTY HISTORICAL MUSEUM, ART LOWE COLLECTION, 1996-100.0007.

Above: Philomath Public School, ca. 1910. Also called West School, it was built in 1900 and had four classrooms. The school was located on west Main Street.

BENTON COUNTY HISTORICAL MUSEUM,
JUSTINA NEWTON THOMAS COLLECTION, 1993-075.0006.

Left: Philomath High School. Built in 1911, this building was located on Seventeenth Street in Philomath until it was destroyed by fire in 1956.

BENTON COUNTY HISTORICAL MUSEUM,
MINNIE McMURTRY COLLECTION, 1994-008.0233.

CHURCHES

Above: First Baptist Church, located at the southeast corner of Fifth and Jefferson streets in Corvallis. Built in 1895, the building was replaced by a new Baptist church in 1917. This church building was moved to First Street, where it was used as a riverfront warehouse for many years. Later, it was moved to the Benton County Fairgrounds, where it is still located. Today, the steeple is missing, and the entrance is at ground level.

BENTON COUNTY HISTORICAL MUSEUM, CORVALLIS PUBLIC LIBRARY COLLECTION. 1985-032-0025L.

AFTER THE FIRST SETTLERS ARRIVED, only a few years elapsed before familiar government, churches, and schools were established. Early Benton County religious denominations reflected the range of beliefs of that period in the United States and its territories. Sometimes, extended family groups from a single congregation or denomination emigrated together, forming their own communities, as was the case with the Methodist Belknap

Settlement in South Benton County and the United Brethren families of the Connor-Kenoyer wagon train of 1853. Before churches were built, these early settlements were served by circuit riders with services held in homes or the local school houses.

In the 1850s, congregations began to build their first churches in Benton County, which were often small, one-story wooden-frame buildings. The only surviving example of a church in this "meeting house" tradition is the North Palestine Baptist Church located on Palestine Road in northeast Benton County.

In the period from the 1860s to the 1880s, many denominations chose Gothic Revival style churches with a central entry and a central bell tower with steeple. Some examples are the Corvallis Presbyterian Church built in the early 1860s, the Monroe Methodist Church (ca. 1865), St. Mary's Catholic Church in Corvallis (1861), St. Rose of Lima Catholic Church in Monroe (1883), Kings Valley Evangelical Church (1877), and probably the Oakridge Presbyterian Church (1879) once located on Bellfountain Road just north of the present Llewellyn Road intersection.

In the 1890s, a second generation of wood-frame churches was built by congregations that had outgrown their pioneer-era churches. These churches, although still made of wood, were larger and often more elaborate than their predecessors, and had side steeples instead of central steeples. As a result of this steeple placement, the facade window treatment was bolder with a large window or grouping of windows. Corvallis Zion Evangelical Lutheran Church, established in 1905, used this design for their 1907 church building on Monroe Avenue.

With increasing population in the more rural areas of Benton County, some congregations divided and built another building. Sometimes the construction of a second church was the result of a rift in the interpretation of theological doctrine. These latter 19th and early 20th century rural churches usually incorporated the side-steeple design although some were the smaller, wood-frame buildings. Examples of this side-steeple design included a Methodist Episcopal Church, the McFarland Church, located four miles north of Monroe (1896); Simpson Memorial Chapel in Alpine (1904); the Union Church at Dusty (Bellfountain), a non-denominational church (1899); the Monroe Methodist Church (1911); the Kings Valley Evangelical Church (early 1890s); and the First United Brethren Church in Christ in Philomath (about 1906).

In the first quarter of the 20th century, most Corvallis denominations replaced their wood-frame churches with large brick or masonry churches. The Presbyterians, who hadn't yet replaced their pioneer-era church, were the first, erecting a brick church on the southwest corner of Eighth and Monroe in 1909. In the teens and twenties most congregations chose classically-inspired designs for their new structures, including the Baptist Church, the First Christian Church, the Congregational Church, and the two Methodist congregations.

Not all church services took place in the confines of a building. Religious camp meetings were held in Benton County in the 19th century. In 1851, the Methodists of the Belknap Settlement held their first camp meeting in a grove on Orin Belknap's land. This meeting was so successful it became an annual event throughout the 19th century. Today this campground is Bellfountain Park.

No.13 M.E. CHURCH MONROE ORE.

Above: Early Wren Community Church, 19th century.
PHOTO DOROTHY BROWN, COURTESY OF MAXINE (HUNTER) BYLER, WREN 2.

Top left: The community of Bellfountain, ca. 1900, with the church in the background. Bellfountain Church, originally known as the Union Church at Dusty (Bellfountain's former name), was built as a non-denominational church in 1899. The church was used by Baptist, United Brethren, and Methodist congregations. The buildings in the foreground are the Bellfountain School, built in 1875, and associated horse sheds.
BENTON COUNTY HISTORICAL MUSEUM, LINDA SEKORA COLLECTION. 1986-131.0027.

Left: Monroe Methodist Church built in 1910-1911 on Orchard Street in Monroe. This church building, which replaced a ca. 1860 wood-frame church in this location, was built by local builder Ernest Brimner, who is particularly well known for the barns he designed and built in southeastern Benton County because of their distinctive hay hoods.
BENTON COUNTY HISTORICAL MUSEUM, HARRIET MOORE COLLECTION. 1994-038.

Below left: Alpine Methodist Church. Built in 1905, the church survived disastrous fires in 1918 and 1924 that virtually leveled the town, only to be burned itself in 1973.
BENTON COUNTY HISTORICAL MUSEUM, HAROLD AND VERNETTA McCALLUM COLLECTION. 1980-034.0046P.

Left: United Brethren in Christ Church in Philomath. This church, built in about 1906, still stands on the southeast corner of Fourteenth and College streets.

BENTON COUNTY HISTORICAL MUSEUM, WILLARD DAVIS COLLECTION, 1990-070.0116.

Below: First Baptist Church located on the northwest corner of Ninth and Monroe streets in Corvallis. This photograph was taken in 1917 shortly after the church's construction. Note the railroad tracks along Ninth Street. This building replaced the wood-frame church built in 1895.

BENTON COUNTY HISTORICAL MUSEUM, EDNA WIESE COLLECTION. 1990-068.0895.

Facing page, top: First Methodist Church formerly located on the northwest corner of Fourth and Madison streets in Corvallis. The photograph was taken in 1897, shortly after the building's construction. After the Methodist congregation moved to its Monroe Street location, the building served as an I.O.O.F. Hall for many years. The church was torn down in 1956 to make way for the J.C. Penney building erected on this site.

BENTON COUNTY HISTORICAL MUSEUM, EDNA WIESE COLLECTION. 1990-068.0407.

Facing page, bottom: Methodist Episcopal Church South located in Corvallis on the southwest corner of Second Street and Van Buren Avenue. This church was erected in 1855 and used until 1897. It has been noted that the design of the church closely copied the 1843 Methodist Episcopal Church in Oregon City, which was reportedly the first Protestant church west of the Rocky Mountains.

BENTON COUNTY HISTORICAL MUSEUM, HARRIET MOORE COLLECTION, 1994-038.

Above: First Congregational Church, once located at the northwest corner of Third and Jefferson streets in Corvallis. The Congregational Church was established in 1883 as the result of a disagreement within the Presbyterian Church. This building was erected in 1889.

BENTON COUNTY HISTORICAL MUSEUM, CORVALLIS PUBLIC LIBRARY COLLECTION. 1985-032.0025A.

Left: This was the first church building erected in the Alsea Valley. In the late 1880s, it served as the Cumberland Presbyterian Church. In the 20th century the building was used by the South Methodist Church and the Baptist Church.

HORNER MUSEUM COLLECTION, 1982-23-1.

Below: St. Mary's Catholic Church, formerly located at the northwest corner of Fourth and Adams. This Mission style church was built in 1912 to replace the wood-frame gothic church erected in 1861 (visible to the right). The old church was moved to this location when the 1912 church was built. This photograph was taken ca. 1940.

BENTON COUNTY HISTORICAL MUSEUM,
PRESTON ONSTAD COLLECTION. 1980-002.0373P.

Above: First Presbyterian Church located on the southwest corner of Eighth and Monroe streets in Corvallis. This building, begun in 1909, replaced a 1860s wood-frame gothic church. Organized in 1853, it was the second Presbyterian congregation in what became the state of Oregon.
BENTON COUNTY HISTORICAL MUSEUM, MARGARET SNYDER JOHNSON ESTATE COLLECTION, 1984-015.0125.

Below: Simpson Chapel (1862) was located on Bellfountain Road approximately halfway between the communities of Alpine and Bellfountain. The congregation was established in the late 1840s by a group of Methodist settlers in this region of the county. The church was built by George and Squire Rycraft, who were well-known as barn builders and lived in Alsea. Both men married young women from Bellfountain.
BENTON COUNTY HISTORICAL MUSEUM, HAROLD AND VERNETTA McCALLUM COLLECTION. 1980-034.0046P.

Facing page: Presbyterian Church built in the early 1860s on the southwest corner of Fourth and Jefferson streets in Corvallis.
Probably taken shortly after the church's construction, this photograph is one of the earliest known photographs of Corvallis.
PHOTO SUBMITTED BY DEAN ALMGREN, GT 35

HOUSES

Right: Drawing of the J.C. and Martha Avery House from an 1859 Kuchel and Dresel lithograph. The house, built for Corvallis' founders, was located on the north side of the Marys River near the present Highway 99 bridges. In 1915, land near the Marys River was purchased for a city park. Descendants of J.C. Avery planned to move the house and preserve it as a landmark. In 1916, however, the house burned before it could be moved. All that remained after the fire were two chimneys, ten feet apart.

BENTON COUNTY HISTORICAL MUSEUM, HARLAND PRATT COLLECTION, 1999-060.0051.

Below: The Charles and Ibby Whiteside House, located at 344 SW 7th Street. Built in 1922, it is an example of a bungalow exhibiting strong oriental influence. Charles Whiteside was a partner in the Whiteside and Locke Hardware store. In the early 1930s, he operated Whiteside Motors, which was located on the corner of Monroe Avenue and Third Street. In 1940, he joined his brothers Sam and George in the theater business.

BENTON COUNTY HISTORICAL MUSEUM, HARRIET MOORE COLLECTION, 1994-038.

Above: The Joseph H. and Effa Wilson House in the 1890s. This house was located on the north side of Jackson Avenue between Seventh and Eighth streets.

BENTON COUNTY HISTORICAL MUSEUM, THOMAS A. WILSON COLLECTION, 1999-063.

Top: The J.S. and Nancy Felger House, located approximately one mile west of Philomath on the south side of U.S. Highway 20. Mr. Felger owned the Marys River Flour Mills. Located near the house, the mill was water-powered from a mill race dug from the Marys River. The house was probably built ca. 1870, shortly after Mr. Felger acquired this property. The house still stands and in more recent years was known as the Neuman House.

BENTON COUNTY HISTORICAL MUSEUM, ARLENE PUGH COLLECTION, 1990-118.0002.

Middle: Mr. and Mrs. John C. Young and their pet cow in front of their residence formerly located at 361 SW Washington Avenue. This photograph was taken ca. 1910. The Safeway store is now located on the site of this house. Note the similarity of the second story doors to those of the J.C. Avery House, and the remodeling that enclosed the porch.

BENTON COUNTY HISTORICAL MUSEUM,
MR. AND MRS. HAROLD LEHNERT COLLECTION, 1981-002.0030P.

Bottom: The James and Mary Watson House, 1934. Located near Hoskins, Oregon, the Watson House was built in the early 1850s by pioneer builder William Pitman. Presently considered the oldest surviving house in Benton County, it was the only building in Benton County recorded by the Historic American Building Survey in the 1930s. The Price family owned this house for much of the 20th century.

HORNER MUSEUM COLLECTION, 6687.

Facing page: The Rev. W.A. Finley and family posing in front of their Gothic Revival style house formerly located at Fifth and Van Buren in Corvallis. W.A. Finley, first president of Corvallis College, lived in this house with his family from 1865 to 1872. Rev. Finley, his wife, his son and niece are standing on the upper story of the porch.

BENTON COUNTY HISTORICAL MUSEUM, HARRIET MOORE COLLECTION, 1994-038.

A KEY COMPONENT
OF BENTON COUNTY'S HISTORY

OREGON STATE
UNIVERSITY

Right: Corvallis College building, ca. 1868. This carte-de-visite photograph of the original college building, built in 1858-59, was taken by the photographers Stryker & Dohse. It is the earliest known photograph of what was to become Oregon State University. In 1868 the campus was located on 5th Street between Madison and Monroe in downtown Corvallis, the same block where Corvallis City Hall is located today.

Stryker and Dohse opened their Corvallis photography gallery in 1868. It was located above B.R. Biddle's drug store on Main Street (now Second Street). Their advertisement in the *Corvallis Gazette* read "Stryker & Dohse, Having permanently established themselves in Corvallis, are prepared to take all kinds of pictures, without regard to weather."

OREGON STATE UNIVERSITY ARCHIVES, HARRIET'S COLLECTION #1344

FROM ITS BEGINNING as a struggling, church-sponsored academy and college to its present stature as one of two Carnegie I Research Institutions in the Pacific Northwest, Oregon State University has exerted a significant influence on the history of Benton County residents, events and places.

OSU traces its roots to 1856, when the Corvallis Academy was founded as the first community school in the Corvallis area. Under the auspices of the Methodist Episcopal Church, South, Corvallis College began offering a four-year, collegiate-level, liberal arts curriculum in 1865. In 1868, through the efforts of Corvallis College faculty member William Walter Moreland, who was also a clerk for the Oregon Legislative Assembly, the state designated Corvallis College as its land grant institution under the provisions of the federal Morrill Act of 1862. The Morrill Act granted Oregon 90,000 acres of land to be used as an endowment to support an agricultural college.

Despite the land grant designation, the small college, under Presidents William A. Finley and Benjamin L. Arnold, constantly struggled financially and with limited enrollment over the next twenty years. The college did purchase a farm (now Lower Campus) with funding from more than 100 local citizens. During this time the college slowly developed curricula that included agriculture, engineering, home economics and military science.

With the passage of the federal Hatch Act in 1887 and second Morrill Act in 1890, additional funds became available to the college. In 1889 the college moved from its downtown Corvallis location to the newly built Administration Building (now Benton Hall) on land adjacent to the college farm.

For the next fifteen years (1892-1907) Presidents John M. Bloss and Thomas M. Gatch directed the college. During this era, several buildings were added to the new campus, a college library was established, intercollegiate athletic competitions began, short courses to farmers were offered, the college newspaper was begun, curricula in forestry and mining were developed, college enrollment grew (from 85 in 1890 to 1,351 in 1908), and international students attended for the first time.

William Jasper Kerr, president for 25 years beginning in 1907, helped to transform the college from a small regional school to one of national importance. During his tenure all aspects of the college expanded significantly. When Kerr took office in 1907, the enrollment stood at approximately 1,300 students and the faculty consisted of 40 members; by 1930 enrollment was more than 3,300 students and the faculty numbered more than 180. He reorganized the academic structure of the college, establishing the schools of Agriculture, Commerce, Engineering and Mechanic Arts, and Domestic Science in 1908, the schools of Forestry and Mining in 1913, the School of Pharmacy in 1917, and the School of Vocational Education and Division of Service Departments in 1918.

Despite financial setbacks and enrollment fluctuations brought on by the Great Depression and a reorganization of higher education in Oregon, Oregon State managed through the 1930s under the leadership of George Peavy. Its "Iron Men" football team of 1933 tied the powerful University of Southern California 0-0 while using only eleven players; it conferred its first doctoral degrees in 1935; and the nucleus of the McDonald Forest in northern Benton County was acquired. During World War II, Oregon State commissioned more cadets than any other non-military institution in the United States and trained 4,812 servicemen as part of the Army Specialized Training Program. Several faculty members served in the armed forces or conducted research directly related to the war effort.

Returning servicemen coming to Oregon State in the years immediately after the war created another enrollment boom (enrollment was nearly 5,900 by 1950), resulting in the hiring of many additional faculty members and the construction of new buildings. Postwar growth continued through the 1950s under President A.L. Strand. New academic and research programs were developed, including several with other countries. And in 1961, Oregon State traded "College" for "University" in its name.

The 1960s, with James H. Jensen as president, were characterized by considerable success in athletics (two football bowl appearances, national championship in cross country in 1961, and seven NCAA track and field individual champions), new degree programs in the humanities and social sciences, and designation as a Sea Grant university. Enrollment doubled, jumping from 7,900 in 1960 to 15,800 in 1968, OSU's centennial year. Robert W. MacVicar led OSU in the 1970s. During the decade several new academic, administrative and student housing buildings were constructed, the departments of Oceanography and Veterinary Medicine became schools, and cultural centers for Native American, Hispanic and African American students opened.

Fluctuations in enrollment and budget defined the 1980s and 1990s at OSU under MacVicar and John L. Byrne, and Paul G. Risser. Despite this uncertainty, new research centers and facilities were added, research grant funds increased by more than 50 percent in the 1990s, several endowed faculty chairs were established, development of distance education programs began, and new academic buildings and a greatly expanded library were constructed. In the late 1990s, OSU adopted a new budget model intended to stabilize its funding, and enrollment was again on the increase.

The photographs in this chapter not only portray the history of OSU but also help define its culture and as a unique community within Benton County. All of the photographs used in this chapter are from the holdings of the Oregon State University Archives.

First graduating class, Corvallis College, 1870. Robert McVeatch, Alice E. Biddle, and James K.P. Currin posed for this portrait by an unknown photographer in the spring of 1870.

McVeatch delivered the valedictory address at the graduation ceremony. He went on to serve two terms in each house of the Oregon legislature and was the 1896 Democratic nominee for Oregon's congressional seat. Biddle was the daughter of B.R. Biddle, the clerk of the college's Board of Trustees and a local druggist. She married William W. Moreland in December of that year; Moreland had been pivotal in Corvallis College's being designated Oregon's land-grant institution in 1868. Little is known of Currin after his graduation from Corvallis College; he was teaching in Missouri in 1873.

OREGON STATE UNIVERSITY ARCHIVES, HARRIET'S COLLECTION #883

Top: Women's basketball team, 1900. The young women in this photo were awarded the "college emblem" for having played two years on the basketball team. They included, from left, Bessie Smith ('01), Letitia Ownsbey ('00), Elizabeth Hoover ('01), Minnie Smith ('03), and Inez Fuller ('00). The coach was Will Beach ('99), the YMCA's physical director. Women's basketball at Oregon State began in 1898; men's basketball did not begin until 1901.

This is one of the earliest photos of women's athletics at OSU. Most team portraits from this time period were taken in a studio or against the side of a building; the women posed among the boulders makes this photograph somewhat rare.
OREGON STATE UNIVERSITY ARCHIVES, P9:8

Middle: Waldo Hall room, 1908. Faye Roadruck (left) and sisters Jessie (center) and Gertrude Davidson study in a room decorated with dance cards, photographs, postcards, pennants, a champion jersey and an OAC pillow. The three women were from Morrow County and lived in Waldo Hall, the new women's dormitory completed in 1908.

Waldo Hall functioned as a dormitory for women until 1959 and then men until 1965, when it was converted to office space.
OREGON STATE UNIVERSITY ARCHIVES, HARRIET'S COLLECTION #36

Bottom: Octagonal barn, ca. 1902. The college's first barn, built in 1889, was this octagonal structure. The addition was built in 1892. It served as the heart of the college's 180-acre farm until 1909, when construction of a new barn was completed. In its later years, the Octagonal Barn served the college as a horse barn, until it burned in September 1924.
OREGON STATE UNIVERSITY ARCHIVES, P90:36

Facing page top: Cadets in front of Benton Hall, ca. 1890. The first building constructed on the original College Farm, now known as Benton Hall, has been the centerpiece of the lower campus ever since. It was erected by the citizens of Benton County under a "Building Association." The cornerstone of the building was laid in August of 1887, and on July 2, 1888, the College Board of Regents took possession of the building. According to the 1892-1893 college catalog, it contained recitation rooms, a chapel, a museum and a library. In 1899, the building received its first major facelift; the brick exterior was cemented over and the east side steps were removed.

In this photograph, college cadets are in formation in front of the building. Notice the Confederate Army style of uniform. In 1872 the college became the first in the Pacific Northwest to offer military instruction.
OREGON STATE UNIVERSITY ARCHIVES, HARRIET'S COLLECTION #38

Facing page bottom: Blacksmith shop, ca. 1892. According to the 1891-1892 college catalog, all second year students in mechanics and mechanical engineering were required to take 5 hours of blacksmithing per week. The work included forging, welding and the making and tempering of tools. The shop was located in the Mechanical Building, which burned in 1898.
OREGON STATE UNIVERSITY ARCHIVES, HARRIET'S COLLECTION #905

Left: William Jasper Kerr delivering President Woodrow Wilson's Declaration of War, April 1917. More than two thousand students, alumni, and faculty of Oregon Agricultural College were enlisted in war service, 71 of whom lost their lives. More than 2,000, in addition, received military training at OAC through the Student Army Training Corps (SATC).

The Bandstand, located on the Library Quad, was a gathering place for campus activities for many years. It was dedicated on June 14, 1910, a gift of the classes of 1908, 1909, 1910 and 1912. The Library (now Kidder Hall) is shown in the background.
OREGON STATE UNIVERSITY ARCHIVES, P25:2901

Below: A bird's eye view of campus, ca. 1911. This view looking to the northwest included the Armory (now McAlexander Fieldhouse), Waldo Hall, Cauthorn (now Fairbanks) Hall, Agriculture Hall (now Strand Agriculture Hall), the Gymnasium (now the Valley Gymnastics Center) and Science (now Education) Hall. Of special note is the railroad side track from the Corvallis and Eastern Railway, which allowed delivery of oil directly to the heating plant, and the south wing of Agriculture Hall, which was under construction at the time. This photograph was originally published as a postcard.
OREGON STATE UNIVERSITY ARCHIVES, HARRIET'S COLLECTION #820

Facing page bottom: A class studying apples, 1909. A variety of classes in pomology and orchard practice were offered to OAC students during the 1909-1910 academic year. Claude Isaac Lewis, the instructor of the class in this photograph (standing), was professor of horticulture at OAC from 1905 to 1920, and served as the Experiment Station's chief horticulturist from 1916 to 1920.
OREGON STATE UNIVERSITY ARCHIVES, HARRIET'S COLLECTION #603

Above: College Librarian Ida A. Kidder sitting in the Reference Room of the new Library, 1918. Kidder is sitting at the second table on the right in this photograph. Affectionately known as "Mother" Kidder, she was OAC's first professionally trained librarian and served as college librarian from 1908 until her death in 1920. Her tenure was a period of unparalleled growth in the Library. Its holdings increased by 800 percent; its staff increased from one position to nine. To accommodate these increases, Kidder planned and oversaw the construction of a new 57,000-square-foot library building costing $158,000. The building was used as Oregon State's Library until 1963, when it was renamed Kidder Hall in memory of Ida Kidder.

OREGON STATE UNIVERSITY ARCHIVES, HARRIET'S COLLECTION #75

Right: Dean of Forestry George Peavy and Fernhoppers in camp, ca. 1920. After a formal forestry curriculum began at OAC in 1906, George Peavy guided the School of Forestry from 1913 through 1940 and developed it into one of the top programs in the nation. Peavy served Oregon State as acting president, 1932-1934, and president, 1934-1940. He later served as mayor of Corvallis. In this photograph, Peavy is sitting on the far left. Fernhoppers was the name used to describe Oregon State's forestry students.

This photograph was taken by Ball Studio, established in Corvallis in 1912. Ball Studio photographers took many photographs of OAC in the 1910s and 1920s.

OREGON STATE UNIVERSITY ARCHIVES, HARRIET'S COLLECTION #849

Left: Mothers and daughters, ca. 1930. Proud mothers visit their daughters at Oregon Agricultural College during a Mothers Weekend in the early 1930s. Kate Wetzel Jameson (second from left) was the much-admired dean of women from 1923 until her retirement in 1941. She was instrumental in establishing Mothers Weekend, which began in 1924 and continues to the present.
OREGON STATE UNIVERSITY ARCHIVES, HARRIET'S COLLECTION #1039

Below: First OAC Band Concert broadcast on college radio station, 1923. On January 25, 1923, the cadet band, under the direction of Captain Harry L. Beard, broadcast a concert including opera, fantasy, popular music and jazz. The 60-piece band was cramped in room 212 in Apperson Hall, which served as the station studio. No acoustic treatment had been applied to the walls, and the microphone (being held on the right) was the type designed for telephone use.

On December 7, 1922, Oregon Agricultural College received a broadcast license for the college's radio station, initially known as KFDJ. In 1925, the call letters were changed to KOAC. KOAC is now a station of the Oregon Public Broadcasting network. OREGON STATE UNIVERSITY ARCHIVES, P95:284

Left: Chancellor William Jasper Kerr and honorary degree recipients; commencement, June 1933. Three honorary degrees were awarded by OSC in 1933, to David C. Henny (second from left), Linus Pauling (center) and Charles A. Howard (right). Dr. Kerr is second from the right and commencement speaker Marvin Gordon Neale is on the left.

Pauling was a 1922 graduate of Oregon State and its most distinguished alumnus. After earning a Ph.D. in chemistry from California Technical Institute in 1925, he went on to win Nobel Prizes in chemistry (1954) and peace (1962).

Dr. William Jasper Kerr served as president of Oregon State from 1907 to 1932, a period of tremendous growth and development for the college. He also served as chancellor of the Oregon State System of Higher Education from 1932 to 1935.
OREGON STATE UNIVERSITY ARCHIVES, HARRIET'S COLLECTION #1578

Right: Women's Building, 1939. Completed in 1926, the Women's Building was designed by architect John V. Bennes of Portland, who designed more than 30 OSU campus buildings constructed between 1907 and 1940. This, however, was his only campus commission as a result of an open competition and is considered by many to be his masterpiece.

Designed as a physical education facility for women, it now houses the College of Health and Human Performance. Classes for both men and women are held in the building. OREGON STATE UNIVERSITY ARCHIVES, P16:94

Below: Bernard Malamud at home, ca. 1960. Novelist Bernard Malamud was an English professor at Oregon State College from 1949 to 1961. During this period he wrote three novels: *The Natural* (1952), *The Assistant* (1957), and *A New Life* (1961) as well as a collection of short stories, *The Magic Barrel* (1959), for which he received the National Book Award. He was presented OSU's Distinguished Service Award in 1969. OREGON STATE UNIVERSITY ARCHIVES, P222

Below right: Commencement procession, June 1952. Since 1950, commencement exercises have been held in Gill Coliseum. One of Oregon State's commencement traditions is the procession of faculty and soon-to-be graduates from the Memorial Union quad to the coliseum. From 1914 until 1949, commencement ceremonies were held in the crowded Men's Gymnasium (Langton Hall).

In the background of the photograph is Weatherford Hall, designed by John Bennes and constructed in 1928 as a men's dormitory.
OREGON STATE UNIVERSITY ARCHIVES, HARRIET'S COLLECTION #492

Above: Launching of the research vessel *Acona* at Newport, Oregon, February 13, 1961. The Oceanography Department's *Acona* was one of the first academic vessels designed specifically for oceanographic research.

Oceanographic research began at Oregon State in 1954 with a $10,000 grant from the Office of Naval Research. The College of Oceanic and Atmospheric Sciences' Ph.D. program was ranked fifth in the nation in 1995 by the National Academy of Sciences.
OREGON STATE UNIVERSITY ARCHIVES, P82:76 NEG. 2524

Top left: Pointers from Coach Gill, 1945. Amory T. "Slats" Gill gave pointers on ball handling to 4-H members attending the 4-H Summer School on the Oregon State College campus. Gill, for whom Gill Coliseum is named, coached the Oregon State University men's basketball team from 1929 to 1964 and is OSU's all-time winningest basketball coach, with 599 wins.

4-H, one of many programs sponsored by the Extension Service at OSU, was established in 1914. The first Boys and Girls 4-H Summer School was held at OAC in June 1916.
OREGON STATE UNIVERSITY ARCHIVES, P146:2450

Middle left: Dean of Home Economics Ava Milam at her desk, March 1950. Ava Milam came to OAC in 1911 and served as dean of the School of Home Economics from 1917 to 1950, perhaps the longest tenure of any school or college dean at Oregon State in the 20th century. During her career, Milam made several trips to Pacific Rim countries, including China, Japan and Korea, to establish or advise home economics programs at universities.
OREGON STATE UNIVERSITY ARCHIVES, HARRIET'S COLLECTION #148

Bottom left: Benny the Beaver and the Rally Squad, 1952. According to the *Barometer*, Benny the Beaver made his live debut on September 18, 1952. Pictured here is Ken Austin, purportedly the first student to don the Benny the Beaver costume.

Benny the Beaver is one of many traditions associated with OSU. Others have included rook lids (which first appeared in 1906), enormous bonfires, spring pageants, and the rook/sophomore tug-of-war.
OREGON STATE UNIVERSITY ARCHIVES, P17:32

Top: Russian language class, ca. 1943. Dean of Science Francois Gilfillan, an accomplished linguist, introduced Russian language study to Oregon State College's foreign languages curriculum in the early 1940s and taught it as part of the Army Specialized Training Program (ASTP) curriculum during World War II. Other languages taught in the ASTP program included Chinese, Portuguese, Spanish, French, and German. From 1943 to 1945, Oregon State taught more than 4,000 ASTP soldiers.

Francois Gilfillan was a 1918 graduate of the OAC School of Pharmacy. He joined the Oregon State faculty in 1927 and served as dean of science from 1939 to 1962. Gilfillan was Oregon State's acting president in 1941 and early 1942.

OREGON STATE UNIVERSITY ARCHIVES, HARRIET'S COLLECTION #935

Middle: A civil handshake between rival coaches, 1962. OSU football coach Tommy Prothro (left) received congratulations from University of Oregon coach Len Casanova after OSU's 20-17 victory in the 1962 Civil War. All-Americans Terry Baker (OSU no. 11) and Steve Barnett (Oregon no. 77) are behind their respective coaches.

Tommy Prothro coached at Oregon State University from 1955 to 1964 and led the Beavers to 63 wins and three bowl games, including two Rose Bowl appearances. Terry Baker was a football All-American, won the 1962 Heisman Trophy, and led Oregon State to a 6-0 win over Villanova in the 1962 Liberty Bowl.

OREGON STATE UNIVERSITY ARCHIVES, P25:3116

Bottom: Black Cultural Center officially opens, 1975. Bobby Hill, president of the Black Student Union, and OSU President Robert W. MacVicar cut the ribbon to officially open OSU's Black Cultural Center. Betty Griffin, an assistant professor of education, was chairperson of the Black Cultural Advisory Board. President MacVicar initiated affirmative action programs for women and minority faculty and students during his administration, from 1970 to 1984.

OREGON STATE UNIVERSITY ARCHIVES, P57:5270

A Pictorial History
of Benton County

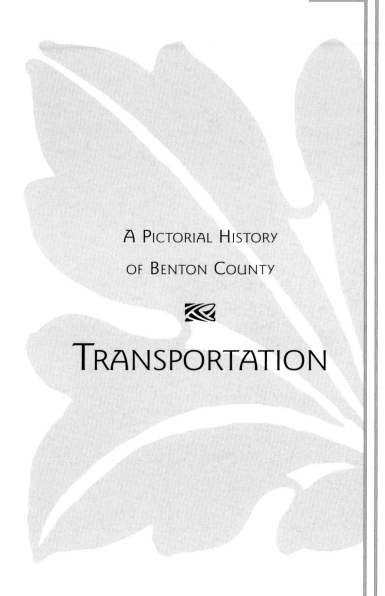

Transportation

IN THE 19TH CENTURY, personal transportation was largely by foot, horseback, or horse-drawn conveyance. In 1852, the Territorial Legislature authorized the Territorial Road from Marysville (now Corvallis) to Winchester. This road roughly followed the current route of Highway 99W through Benton County, and in 1866, with a land grant from the federal government, the Corvallis and Yaquina Bay Military Wagon Road was completed. Stagecoach service was established through Benton County the 1850s, and in 1860 the California Stage Company began offering service from Portland to Sacramento. The Eglin Stage Company, the local stage stop and stables, was located on the southeast corner of Third and Madison in Corvallis.

Prior to the construction of bridges, ferries were used to cross Benton County's larger rivers, such as the Willamette at Corvallis and the Long Tom River in Monroe. In 1853, J.C. Avery operated a ferry across the Marys River, but in 1856 it was replaced by a toll bridge.

In 1851, a steamboat ascended the Willamette River as far as Corvallis for the first time. Situated at the head of navigation on the Willamette River for many years, Corvallis became the headquarters for those traveling to the mines of southern Oregon and California in the 1850s. During the 1860s and 1870s, when wheat was the primary crop of the region, Willamette River steamboat transportation reached its height. After 1880, when rail lines began to serve Benton County, the river played less of a role in the economic life of the county. Willamette River steamboats were still used in the latter part of the 19th century, but as the century progressed, they became increasingly less important for transporting freight. Passenger service, providing pleasure rides up and down the Willamette, however, became fashionable at this time.

The Western Oregon Railway Company completed a rail line to Corvallis late in 1879 with the first passenger train arriving in Corvallis from Portland on January 28, 1880. The trip took nine hours, requiring refueling of wood every ten miles. In 1908, a rail line was extended south of Corvallis with the incorporation of the Corvallis and Alsea River Railway. In 1911, the line was purchased, renamed the Portland, Eugene, and Eastern Railway, and extended from Monroe to Eugene.

The Oregon and Pacific Railroad from Corvallis to Yaquina City, located on Yaquina Bay east of Newport, was completed in December of 1884. Here, in conjunction with ocean-going steamers, freight and passenger service was established with San Francisco. In 1887, the Oregon and Pacific Railroad was extended east to Albany with a plan to cross the Cascades and link up with an eastern route at Boise City. Capital, however, was lacking and the railroad went into receivership in 1891. Construction had reached the current Detroit Dam area by 1893. In 1895, the railroad was purchased by A.B. Hammond for his lumber interests. Numerous logging railroads were also constructed in Benton County in the early years of the 20th century to tap the timber resources of the Coast Range.

In 1889 the Corvallis Street Railway was incorporated, and in November of 1890 it was reported that the contractor had completed the car lines to the depots and put in the switches—making a total of 10,828 feet of street railway in the city. Corvallis now ranked third in the state outside of Portland in the extent of its street railways. The street railway operated with three cars, each carrying about 12 passengers, pulled by two horses. The street cars were not as successful as hoped. One of the drivers noted years later that the street cars were the subject of jokes for miles around, apparently because they were always coming off the track. For several years, the street cars were used only as hotel buses to meet the trains—until the tracks were taken up in 1902.

The first inter-urban train to serve Corvallis was the Oregon Electric in 1912. Located on the east side of the Willamette River, trains traveled from Portland to Eugene. In order to serve Corvallis, a spur line was built to the eastern foot of the Van Buren Street Bridge where a depot was built. With the success of the Oregon Electric, Southern Pacific decided to electrify its west side line, and in 1917 Benton County residents could climb aboard the "Red Electric," named for the steel cars that were painted a bright red, and travel to Portland. Passenger trains were doomed, however, by the increasing popularity and affordability of the automobile. In 1929, inter-urban train service ceased.

The first decades of the 20th century saw sweeping changes in transportation modes and networks. Benton County saw the end of the steamboat era, the rise and fall of inter-urban railroads, the first airplane, and the introduction of the automobile.

One of the first Benton County residents to own a car was August Fischer of Corvallis, who purchased a Rambler in 1903. Mark Rickard, another early car owner, was the first to sell cars in Benton County, initially in the back of Long's Sporting Goods Store on Second Street. In 1908, Mr. Rickard built an automobile sales

garage on the southeast corner of Second and Van Buren streets in Corvallis, the town's first. Construction of numerous automobile-related businesses in Benton County followed. There were 14 automobile service stations in Corvallis in 1934. In rural Benton County, gas pumps appeared in front of local general stores, and new service stations were erected at crossroad locations.

Among the most important road projects of the early 20th century was the construction of the Pacific Coast Highway, which extended from Vancouver, British Columbia, to San Diego, California. The highway had two routes in the Willamette Valley: one on the east side of the Willamette River and one on the west side. Corvallis and Monroe were on the west side route, which was completed in 1923 and today is known as Highway 99W.

Above: Corvallis and Eastern Railway Station at Philomath. The Oregon Central and Eastern Railway, renamed Corvallis and Eastern in 1897, took over the financially troubled Oregon and Pacific Railroad in 1894. This depot, located just north of the intersection of Pioneer and Fifteenth streets, was used for freight as well as for passenger service. A favorite destination was the Oregon coast.
BENTON COUNTY HISTORICAL MUSEUM, JAMES McMURTRY COLLECTION, 1994-008.0389.

No. 2000 TRESSEL AND TUNNEL AT SUMIT ONCE RY TO NEW PORT OREGON.

Above: Southern Pacific Lines three-car Red Electric train on Sixth Street, Corvallis, ca. 1920. The high school is in the background on what is now Central Park, and the railroad depot is to the left. The man in the center is William Alnutt.

PHOTO SUBMITTED BY ROBERT R. LOWRY, GT 19.

Left: Trestle and tunnel at the summit on the Corvallis and Eastern Railroad on the route to Newport, Oregon. Passenger excursion trains to the coast were popular in the early 20th century.

BENTON COUNTY HISTORICAL MUSEUM, HARRIET MOORE COLLECTION, 1994-038.

Above: Moving the Corvallis railroad depot in 1917. The depot was moved to its second location on the east side of Sixth Street between Madison and Monroe avenues. This new location was selected because the depot was to serve the new electric interurban service initiated in 1917. The depot was used by the railroad until 1946 when it was transferred to the City of Corvallis. This building served as the Corvallis Police Station for many years. In 1982, it was moved to its present location on the Willamette River and became Michael's Landing. BENTON COUNTY HISTORICAL MUSEUM, WAMPLER FAMILY COLLECTION, 1996-046.0012.

Facing page top: Southern Pacific's Union Depot in Corvallis. The building in the foreground in the Wells Fargo Express office. This photograph, taken sometime in the 1910s, shows the depot in its original location near Ninth Street and Washington Avenue. Built in 1910, the depot was in this location for only seven years before being relocated to Sixth Street. The Wells Fargo building remains on Sixth Street where it is still owned by the city.

BENTON COUNTY HISTORICAL MUSEUM, HARRIET MOORE COLLECTION, 1994-038.

Facing page middle: Train in front of the Oregon and Pacific depot in Corvallis. Now located near Seventh and Washington, the depot, completed in 1887, is believed to be the oldest wood-frame, two-story depot in Oregon. It is listed in the National Register of Historic Places. BENTON COUNTY HISTORICAL MUSEUM, HARRIET MOORE COLLECTION, 1994-038.

Facing page bottom: Train depot at Wellsdale. This town, originally known as Wells, was destroyed in 1942 for the construction of Camp Adair, a World War II Army training facility. The photograph illustrates the power lines for the interurban electric trains, which ran between Portland and Eugene from 1917 to 1929.

BENTON COUNTY HISTORICAL MUSEUM, VELMA RAWIE COLLECTION, 1983-089.0002.

Above: Railroad construction crew working on the line of the Oregon and Pacific Railroad. The Oregon Pacific Railroad, which was completed in December of 1884, connected Corvallis and Yaquina City, which was located on Yaquina Bay east of Newport.

BENTON COUNTY HISTORICAL MUSEUM, FRENCH BUTLER ESTATE COLLECTION, 1992-023.0005.

Right: The last train on First Street, before the rails were removed in the 1950s.

PHOTO SUBMITTED BY JEAN MATER, GT 20.

Top: Depot at Monroe, Oregon. In 1908, railroad tracks extended south of Corvallis for the first time. This line, known as the Corvallis and Alsea Railway, was acquired by Southern Pacific in 1912. Southern Pacific extended this line south of Monroe, thereby connecting Corvallis and Eugene by rail. Passenger service to Eugene was discontinued in 1938 and the tracks south of Monroe were removed.

BENTON COUNTY HISTORICAL MUSEUM,
VERNETTA AND HAROLD McCALLUM COLLECTION, 1980-034.0004P.

Middle: Covered bridge once located on Bellfountain Road just south of Philomath. The span crossed the Marys River.

BENTON COUNTY HISTORICAL MUSEUM,
JAMES McMURTRY COLLECTION, 1994-008.0529M.

Bottom: Rare photograph of plank road off of First Street leading to the Corvallis ferry, which was located where the Van Buren Street bridge now crosses the Willamette River. The plank road descended the bank parallel to First Street.

BENTON COUNTY HISTORICAL MUSEUM,
FLOSSIE OVERMAN COLLECTION, 1986-059.132Y.

Top: Willamette River ferry at Corvallis, 1907. The ferry was located in the same general location as the present Van Buren Street bridge.

BENTON COUNTY HISTORICAL MUSEUM, HARRIET MOORE COLLECTION, 1994-038.

Middle: Irish Bend ferry operator, Tune "Pop" Rictor and a group of local ladies crossing the Willamette, 1939-1941. "Pop" was the last Irish Bend ferry operator.

PHOTO SUBMITTED BY JOE RICTOR, GT 27.

Bottom: "Steamer *Altona* on Corvallis Dock." The steamboat is tied at the wharf located between Jefferson and Madison avenues. The photograph was probably taken in the 1890s.

BENTON COUNTY HISTORICAL MUSEUM, HARRIET MOORE COLLECTION, 1994-038.

Facing page: Steamer *Grahamona* at a Corvallis wharf sometime after 1913. Minerva Kiger Reynolds, in her book, *Corvallis in 1900*, recounts that steamboat excursions down the river and back were a diversion for local residents. A chicken dinner was served, and the band provided music. In 1900 the fare was $1.50.

BENTON COUNTY HISTORICAL MUSEUM, HARRIET MOORE COLLECTION, 1994-038.

Right: Street grader during a Fourth of July parade, early 1900s. This particular machine belonged to Adolph Leder. The engineer was Henry Oetjen. On the wheel was Mr. Butschek. Others in the picture include Charles Summers, John Stahl, Jacob Leder, Robert Leder, Mrs. Manuel Meier, and Mrs. Henry Gerding.

PHOTO SUBMITTED BY THE GERDING FAMILY AND SHELDON MEIER, GT 23.

Below: On June 10, 1952, for the first time in 25 years, the swing span bridge over the Willamette River at Corvallis was opened to permit a boat to pass upstream. The boat was the Army Corps of Engineers snag boat *Monticello*. (MIKE BRADLEY, PHOTOGRAPHER)

BENTON COUNTY HISTORICAL MUSEUM, HARRIET MOORE COLLECTION, 1994-038.

Above: "New Steel Bridge, Corvallis, Oregon." This bridge, commonly called the Van Buren Street Bridge, still spans the Willamette River. It was built in 1913, replacing a ferry in that location. The sign on the bridge reads, "$25.00 fine for riding or driving over this bridge faster than a walk or for driving on this bridge at one time more than 25 head of cattle or horses." This bridge is still in use today.

BENTON COUNTY HISTORICAL MUSEUM, ART LOWE COLLECTION, 1996-100.0015.

Left: Horse-drawn streetcar in front of the Occidental Hotel in the 1890s. The Occidental was located at the southeast corner of Second Street and Madison Avenue.

BENTON COUNTY HISTORICAL MUSEUM, HARRIET MOORE COLLECTION, 1994-038.

Top: Buggy ride in the early 20th century. The lettering on the side of the wagon reads "Huston and Bogue, Corvallis Oregon." Robert Huston and William Bogue were partners in a Corvallis hardware store.

BENTON COUNTY HISTORICAL MUSEUM, EDNA WIESE COLLECTION, 1990-068.1340.

Middle: Freight team of W.H. Malone, owner of the former Moses Bros. store in Alsea. N.C. Pickett is the teamster in this photograph taken on the north side of the Moses Bros. store in Philomath.

BENTON COUNTY HISTORICAL MUSEUM, BILL FENDALL COLLECTION, 1981-106.0022P.

Bottom: Inside the Eglin Livery Stable. This stable was located near the southeast corner of Third and Madison streets in Corvallis.

BENTON COUNTY HISTORICAL MUSEUM, EDNA WIESE COLLECTION, 1990-068.1269.

Facing page top: The interior of Rickard's Garage in Corvallis, ca. 1910. Note the similar appearance of this early auto garage and the photograph of the Eglin livery stable. Mr. Rickard established the first automobile agency in Corvallis. Built in 1908, this garage, located at the southeast corner of Second and Van Buren, was destroyed by fire in 1923.

BENTON COUNTY HISTORICAL MUSEUM, MARIE READ COLLECTION, 1982-021.0004P.

Facing page bottom: David C. Fendall, salesman for the Whiteside Chevrolet Garage in Corvallis. Reportedly, he would drive a new car to either Alsea, Siletz or Newport, sell the car, and walk back to Corvallis.

BENTON COUNTY HISTORICAL MUSEUM, BILL FENDALL COLLECTION, 1981-106.0037.

Above: Dodge truck hauling a "one-log load" and automobile in the late 1940s in Benton County.
BENTON COUNTY HISTORICAL MUSEUM, JIM AND OLETA HEDRIC COLLECTION, 1999-105.

Below: Frank Plunkett at the "Y" Station in Philomath in the 1930s. This gas station was located at the intersection of State Highways 20 and 34. The office for the Philomath Auto Park is visible on the right side of the photograph.
BENTON COUNTY HISTORICAL MUSEUM, JAMES McMURTRY COLLECTION, 1994-008.0383.

A PICTORIAL HISTORY
OF BENTON COUNTY

EVENTS

Aside from Christmas, the Fourth of July was the biggest day of the year. There was always a hot time in Corvallis on that day. People living in the country came for miles...It usually began with a twenty-one gun salute...The whole town was decorated...Firecrackers popped...There were runaways, fires, and accidents, but nothing stopped the celebration.

Minerva Kiger Reynolds

THE FOURTH OF JULY tradition of a parade, competitions of all kinds, and a formal program continued well into the 20th century. It is no surprise that the Fourth of July was chosen as the date to lay the cornerstone for the new Benton County Courthouse in 1888. The old courthouse was in good condition, but it was small and crowded. Civic leaders felt a larger and more dignified structure would better suit their fast-growing community.

World events often shaped the local community's celebrations. Shortly after midnight on November 11, 1918, the firebell

began to ring. Firemen came on the run to learn that an armistice had been signed with Germany, and World War I was officially over. The fire bell continued to ring "like the day of judgment." Soon church bells began to chime, and the town of Corvallis was awake! The parade held later in the morning was the "largest ever seen in a town that had seen some whoppers." Dr. William Jasper Kerr, President of Oregon Agricultural College, declared that the day would become as important at the Fourth of July.

Above: Corvallis residents viewing the flood of 1890. The covered bridge over the Marys River in Corvallis can be seen on the right side of the photograph.
BENTON COUNTY HISTORICAL MUSEUM, HARRIET MOORE COLLECTION, 1994-038.

Sirens, bells, firecrackers, and horns marked the beginning of the celebration of V-J Day on August 14, 1945. World War II was officially over! Local citizens and members of the military hurriedly organized an impromptu parade. Quickly decorated cars led the parade followed by a group of sailors, Oregon State College students and band, the Gray Ladies and the Red Cross ambulance, the high school band, the American Legion drum corps and band, representatives of the Legion and the Veterans of Foreign Wars, and many other groups. Scores of shouting civilians followed in trucks and cars. The parade began shortly after 6 p.m., and one hour later the groups were still marching. Long after the parade, crowds milled around the downtown, and dancing in front of the courthouse lasted until 1:30 in the morning. "Hilarious, noisy, but sane," was the official opinion of the spontaneous celebration.

Sometimes world events were no cause for celebrating. On September 27, 1881 a memorial service was held for James A. Garfield, the 20th president of the United States, who died as the result of an assassin's bullet. In his opening remarks, Judge Kelsay said, "Party spirit sleeps this day throughout the length and breadth of this vast nation."

Catastrophic weather and fires are long remembered and often recorded. David Fagan's 1885 *History of Benton County*, describes a "hurricane" that "visited" the state on January 9, 1880. While no one was injured, farmers suffered the most. Fences were flattened; barns, sheds, and farm machinery were demolished. Grain and hay were destroyed, bridges damaged, and roads blocked by fallen trees.

Since Corvallis is located on the banks of the Willamette River, floods have played an important role in its history. The 1861 December flood severely damaged the town of Orleans across the river from Corvallis. Both communities were in the same strategic position—at the head of navigation on the Willamette River. Residents of Orleans woke to the sound of drift logs striking against their homes. No lives were lost, but like several other riverboat towns including Champoeg, Orleans never recovered. Another newsmaker was the flood of 1874, but it was the flood of 1875—a minor one—that caused the re-routing of the main channel of the Willamette, and created a new waterway—Booneville Channel. Named for the village of Booneville, a mile south of Corvallis, it was one of the few accessible shipping points in a wide, often marshy, area of bottomland. Booneville was left with a lessening of water, and shipments waited for the favorable seasons of highwater—winter or spring. About the same time, river traffic began to diminish as the railroad provided more reliable shipping. Less and less effort was made to keep the channel clear and passable, and soon Booneville passed into history. The floods of 1890 and 1894 were also memorable. Perhaps, it was one of these floods that generated the story that the water got so high logs floated on the courthouse lawn.

"Willamette on the Rampage," reported *The Weekly Gazette Times*, on a flood that halted many Thanksgiving Day celebrations in 1909. Buildings and basements near the river were flooded. A carload or more of lumber at the site of the McCready Mill began to float away, although "most of it was captured." Reminiscing about that day, H.G. Hastie commented, "We didn't have much to be thankful about..."

The "worst flood in history" occurred on New Year's Day 1943, when three people lost their lives, property damage ran "into the millions of dollars," and hundreds of heads of livestock were lost. Many people were rescued from the floodwaters, and the Army Corps of Engineers, still stationed at Camp Adair, set up headquarters at the junior high school and helped with the rescue operations.

Fires figure prominently in the history of the county. Alpine suffered two disastrous fires in 1918 and 1924, each one virtually leveling the town. After the second fire, the town never achieved prosperity again. Fires plagued the wood-frame structures in Corvallis in 1869, 1873, 1875, and 1883, often destroying many buildings in the downtown. In the early 1920s, fire destroyed the Rickard Garage. Mark Rickard, the first automobile dealer in Benton County, built a new one in the same location. Fire gutted the interior of the Whiteside Theatre in 1927, and in 1936 another fire caused damage to its roof and ceiling. Both times the theatre was restored to its original splendor. A fire in 1946 destroyed the Corvallis Junior High School located in today's Central Park. For the first time in 75 years there was no school building in this location.

Of all the fires, only one took a life. On February 25, 1882, a warehouse near the railroad depot caught fire. George P. Wrenn died instantly when a beam fell on him as he helped move the contents out of the building. Wrenn had helped form the first fire company in Corvallis, and served two terms as the Chief Engineer of the Corvallis Fire Department.

Above: Train wreck, which occurred between Philomath and Corvallis in the early 20th century.
BENTON COUNTY HISTORICAL MUSEUM COLLECTION, 1989-006.0022.

Right: Collapse of the bridge over the Marys River in 1932. The Marys River bridge fell 30 feet into the river carrying the car of Bernie Hadenfeld. Hadenfeld escaped death when a huge steel girder fell across the rumble seat a few inches from the driver's seat as his car was thrown down with the bridge.
BENTON COUNTY HISTORICAL MUSEUM, EDNA WIESE COLLECTION, 1990-068.1328.

Top: View of the flood of 1890 from the roof of the Benton County Courthouse. The Willamette River stretches to the east as far as the eye can see. Houses on First Street in Corvallis, however, are above the high water.

BENTON COUNTY HISTORICAL MUSEUM,
ARTHUR L. LOWE COLLECTION, 1996-100.0003.

Middle: Flood at Corvallis in 1923. Photograph looks east from the east end of the Van Buren Street Bridge toward the Oregon Electric Station. Water from this flood eventually ran through the depot windows.

BENTON COUNTY HISTORICAL MUSEUM,
JOHN GARMAN COLLECTION, 1980-093.0002P.

Bottom: 1895 train wreck at tunnel #3. The wreck occurred on April 29, 1895, killing conductor John Campbell of Corvallis and brakeman Grant Wilcox of Albany. The train, which came to rest in the Yaquina River, consisted of fourteen boxcars loaded with freight for San Francisco (to be transported by steamer from Yaquina Bay). The engine made it across the bridge; the men killed, however, were standing on an empty flatcar as the bridge gave way.

BENTON COUNTY HISTORICAL MUSEUM,
HARRIET MOORE COLLECTION, 1994-038.

Above: Whiteside Theater fire, October 1, 1936. *The Gorgeous Hussy* with Joan Crawford was playing on the screen when flames erupted between the roof and ceiling at 8:40 P.M. A passerby on Madison Avenue alerted theater workers, who then evacuated theater patrons in an orderly manner. There were no injuries. The Whiteside Brothers used the Majestic Theater until repairs were completed.

BENTON COUNTY HISTORICAL MUSEUM, HARLAND PRATT COLLECTION, 1989-011.0024.

Facing page top: Aftermath of a 1911 fire that destroyed a sawmill on the Willamette River near Second Avenue and Polk Street. A sawmill had been in this location since 1854 and this was the third one destroyed by fire. The 1854 sawmill was destroyed in 1868. The rebuilt mill burned in 1889.

BENTON COUNTY HISTORICAL MUSEUM, HARRIET MOORE COLLECTION, 1983-019.0053.

Facing page middle: Aftermath of the Rickard Garage fire on September 6, 1923. The Rickard Garage, located at the southeast corner of Second Street and Van Buren Avenue, was built in 1908 and was the first building in Benton County specifically built for automobile service and sales. The fire was ignited when an electrical spark came in contact with gas from a leaking tank. The fire also destroyed three nearby residences on First Street. The automobile garage presently at this location was built by Mark Rickard to replace the one destroyed by fire.

BENTON COUNTY HISTORICAL MUSEUM, EDNA WIESE COLLECTION, 1990-068.1568.

Facing page bottom: Corvallis Junior High School Fire, 1946. This building, located in what is now Central Park, was erected in 1909-1910 as Corvallis High School. When the present Corvallis High School was built in 1935, this building was converted to a junior high.

BENTON COUNTY HISTORICAL MUSEUM, HARRIET MOORE COLLECTION, 1994-038.

Above top: Corvallis Parade on Second Street, ca. 1910.
BENTON COUNTY HISTORICAL MUSEUM, RUTH CAIN COLLECTION, 1989-037.0001.

Above bottom: Corvallis city band on Second Street, between Madison and Jefferson, ca. 1900.
PHOTO SUBMITTED BY ROBERT ADAMS, GT1.

Right: Arch dedicated to returning World War I soldiers, sailors and marines in 1919. Pictured are Corvallis firemen and auxiliary who designed and constructed the arch. (BALL STUDIO PHOTOGRAPH)
BENTON COUNTY HISTORICAL MUSEUM, MR. AND MRS. HOWARD LUTZ COLLECTION, 1982-071.0001P.

WELCOME

ARCH DEDICATED AS
LOVING TRIBUTE OF WELCOME AND HONOR
BENTON COUNTY'S RETURNING SOLDIERS
SAILORS AND MARINES.

© 1919
BALL STUDIO
CORVALLIS ORE.

CORVALLIS FIREMEN AND AUXILLIARY
GNED AND CONSTRUCTED THE ARCH

Above: "Recruit Chaser," Navy recruiting efforts in downtown Corvallis in 1918. The photograph is taken near the corner of Second Street and Madison Avenue. J.C. Lowe, then Corvallis mayor, and Walter H. Kline occupy the front seat of the open touring automobile. The hood ornament appears to be a real stuffed eagle. Visible across the street from the Benton State Bank Building is the Occidental Hotel (right side of photograph), which was demolished to make room for the present hotel building on that site. (BALL STUDIO PHOTOGRAPH)

BENTON COUNTY HISTORICAL MUSEUM, ARTHUR L. LOWE COLLECTION, 1999-128.0004.

Right: Corvallis firemen participate in the V.E. Day parade in downtown Corvallis at the corner of Third and Madison on May 8, 1945.

PHOTO SUBMITTED BY PATTI JANEGO, GT 17.

Left: Philomath Frolic Parade in the late 1950s. The intersection in the background is Thirteenth and Main streets.

BENTON COUNTY HISTORICAL MUSEUM, ELLIE WEST COLLECTION, 1985-148.0005.

Below: Dedication of the Fort Hoskins Memorial on May 30, 1922. Two hundred people attended this event to place a stone monument dedicating the fort, which was established in 1856 and abandoned in 1866. Situated in the present day community of Hoskins, the fort's location was designed to prevent the incursion of white settlers onto the newly established Siletz Indian Reservation, and to keep the Indians confined to the reservation. Lieutenant Philip H. Sheridan, known for his service during the Civil War, served at Fort Hoskins for several months.
(BALL STUDIO PHOTOGRAPH)

BENTON COUNTY HISTORICAL MUSEUM, HARRIET MOORE COLLECTION, 1992-041.0054G.

Right: The Corvallis 1957 Centennial parade as seen from Second Street in front of Montgomery Ward store.

PHOTO SUBMITTED BY JOHN DOUGHERTY, GT 12.

Below: Then-vice president Richard Nixon visiting Corvallis in the mid-1950s.

BENTON COUNTY HISTORICAL MUSEUM, T. MICHAEL BRADLEY COLLECTION, 1992-049.0014.

A PICTORIAL HISTORY
OF BENTON COUNTY

AT WORK

IN THE 1800s, farming was the primary occupation and the main means of livelihood for most Benton County men. Of the 150 men chosen for jury duty in early Benton County, 140 were farmers—93 percent. Few women in the early history of the county worked outside the home, and if they did it was usually in a husband's business.

The first Benton County businesses were small in the 1900s, and usually run by family members. Oregon State Agricultural College in Corvallis was not a large employer. There were not many additional jobs in the local stores either, but surrounding farms provided some work.

Hop-raising had become an industry, and many were employed picking hops. Hop yard owners provided camping grounds for their pickers, and ran a daily wagon into Corvallis for workers who did not wish to camp. The standard wage for hop picking was a penny a pound. A basketful—called a box—weighed 50 pounds. Whole families

picked hops—women averaged three or four boxes a day, children one or two, and men five or six. So a family might earn six or seven dollars a day, and those were good wages in a time when a man earned a dollar a day, or a dollar and a half if he brought his own lunch.

By 1900, the timber industry was becoming very important. Steam power had come to the woods in the form of the steam donkey that pulled logs to a central point. Steam locomotives could haul very large loads over long distances, and hundreds of miles of railroad tracks were laid into the forests and connected with the main lines in the valley. After taking all the trees from one area, loggers moved to a new place, along with the logging camp buildings, which were loaded onto the train. Trucks were developed to haul large loads and they gradually began to replace the logging railroads as trucking was cheaper and more efficient, and roads could be built more easily to areas previously inaccessible.

Demand for wood during World War I accelerated timber harvesting. However, the Great Depression hit the industry hard, closing lumber camps and dropping annual timber production. World War II again created a tremendous demand for wood products, making lumber more valuable, and in 1942, for the first time, the money an owner received for logged trees was often enough to replant a harvested area.

During World War II, Camp Adair provided 1,300 civilian jobs filled by people in nearby communities. The large payroll proved a boon to local merchants, who also supplied goods and services to the camp. It was a time when women joined the work force in large numbers because men were not available; frequently they filled non-traditional jobs. After the war, when the men returned home and jobs were not as plentiful, women were forced to return to homemaking and other "women's work." However, as the cost of living climbed, women began returning to the work force, and many young women hoped to have a career before they married and started a family.

Women were not a large percentage of the paid work force in the early 20th century. Teaching, nursing, clerking, and stenography were accepted professions for women at the time. In 1914—25 years after the courthouse opened—the county finally acknowledged that women used the courthouse, too, and added a restroom for them in the basement. Women were employed at the courthouse during this time, but the first woman elected to public office was Susan Beeson Taylor. She served as Benton County Treasurer from 1921 until her death in 1948. Oregon State Agricultural College, now a university—a land, sea, and space grant institution—employed more and more people as the scope of its programs increased and enrollment grew. Currently, it is the county's largest employer, followed by manufacturing, government, trade, services, and agriculture. Agriculture, timber, and rock materials are still the county's three primary natural resources. While these resources continue to have economic importance, with the arrival of Hewlett-Packard in the mid-1970s, a growing high-tech industry has emerged.

Top: Threshing grain in the 1870s or 1880s. The horse, on an inclined treadmill, supplied the power to operate the threshing machine.

BENTON COUNTY HISTORICAL MUSEUM, BUMP FAMILY COLLECTION, 1998-083.0016.

Middle: Harvesting hops in Benton County, ca. 1935. For decades, Oregon was the largest producer of hops in the United States. When harvest time arrived, many Benton County families headed to the fields where they camped and picked hops.

BENTON COUNTY HISTORICAL MUSEUM, HARLAND PRATT COLLECTION, 1981-056.0001P.

Bottom: The threshing crew at harvest time near Philomath, Oregon, ca. 1900.

BENTON COUNTY HISTORICAL MUSEUM, JUSTINA NEWTON THOMAS COLLECTION, 1996-064.0055.

Above: Top, harvest crew with steam-powered thrashing machine, Bellfountain 1906. Bottom, Chuck wagon. Pictured from left to right are Ebby Wilson, unknown boy, Bill Stanturf, Lawn Wilkenson, Walter Poole, Everett Hanshaw, Norm Miller, Marvin Coon, Dow boy, Ivan Rickard, Mother Coon, Pearl Coon, Chris Hanshaw, and Dale Perin.
PHOTO SUBMITTED BY ALVAH HINTON, GT 16.

Left: Steam donkey and loggers in the Kings Valley area ca. 1895. The donkey—powered by steam, gas, diesel, or electricity—was used to haul logs from the woods, to load logs at landings, and move equipment. At one time 26 different types of steam donkey were built in the Pacific Northwest by one firm alone. (ORIGINAL PHOTOGRAPH BY J.F. FORD, PORTLAND, OREGON)
BENTON COUNTY HISTORICAL MUSEUM, HOWARD ATKESON COLLECTION, 1995-052.0004.

Above: Horse logging for the Benton County Lumber Company in the early 20th century. Instead of using machines, horses were sometimes used for skidding—hauling logs to the landing to be loaded.

BENTON COUNTY HISTORICAL MUSEUM, CORVALLIS PUBLIC LIBRARY COLLECTION, 1985-032.0025AB.

Facing page: Felling a tree in Benton County in the early 20th century. The loggers are standing on springboards that give them good footing when the ground is too rough or steep, or when the tree has a large flaring base.

BENTON COUNTY HISTORICAL MUSEUM, CORVALLIS PUBLIC LIBRARY COLLECTION, 1985-032.0026BM.

Below: Log train on the Noon tracks. The Noon Railroad was built ca. 1905 by the Noon Lumber Company and traveled up the Woods Creek drainage to tap the rich timber stands on the north side of Marys Peak. Cab of engine reads "Noon Lumber Co."

BENTON COUNTY HISTORICAL MUSEUM, MINNIE McMURTRY ESTATE COLLECTION, 1994-008.0341.

Above: Philip Weber Furniture Store on Second Street, ca. 1900.
BENTON COUNTY HISTORICAL MUSEUM, HARRIET MOORE COLLECTION, 1994-038.

Right: Corvallis Independent Telephone wagon on Second Street in the first decade of the 20th century. Due to popular demand, the Independent Telephone Company had to install an additional switchboard in January 1909 that would allow another 2,000 subscribers to receive telephones. Their old switchboard had a capacity for only 600, but actually accommodated 700.
BENTON COUNTY HISTORICAL MUSEUM, ARTHUR L. LOWE COLLECTION, 1999-128.0016.

Above: Corvallis telephone operator Margaret Livingston Lowe in the early 20th century. In 1912, Corvallis claimed to have more phones per capita than any other city its size.
BENTON COUNTY HISTORICAL MUSEUM, ARTHUR L. LOWE COLLECTION, 1999-128.0007.

Top left: "Sunny" Jim Patton worked as a bootblack (ca. 1920) in a local barbershop. BENTON COUNTY HISTORICAL MUSEUM, BILL FENDALL COLLECTION, 1981-106.0052P.

Middle left: W.W. Wright, business and math teacher at Philomath College, with a business student in 1928 or 1929. The college, which opened in 1867, closed in 1929.
BENTON COUNTY HISTORICAL MUSEUM, HARRIET DINGUS COLLECTION, 1988-100.0033.

Bottom left: Hamburger Inn, 1930, located on Twelfth and Jefferson, in Corvallis. Staff pictured from left to right are Hazel, Bill, and Tina Coon.
PHOTO SUBMITTED BY LINDA OLSEN, GT 36

Above top: The O.K. Barber Shop in Corvallis in the 1920s. Operated by Slim Hutchinson and David Fendall, the shop was located in the Rennie-Allen Building on Madison Avenue—the present location of the Shoe Hutch. BENTON COUNTY HISTORICAL MUSEUM, BILL FENDALL COLLECTION, 1981-106.0051P

Above bottom: Inside the Corvallis Meat Company in 1922 or 1923. The Corvallis Meat Company was located in the Taylor Building, 136 SW Second Street.
BENTON COUNTY HISTORICAL MUSEUM, HARRIET MOORE COLLECTION, 1982-004.0013P.

Above left: Inside the Western Oregon Packing Corporation's cannery on Ninth Street in Corvallis, ca. 1925. Located where the Cannery Mall is today, there was a cannery at this location until the early 1970s.
(PHOTOGRAPH BY BALL STUDIO) BENTON COUNTY HISTORICAL MUSEUM, HARRIET MOORE COLLECTION, 1982-004.0072P

Left: This photograph of Corvallis High School students gardening appeared in the 1915 *Chintimini*, the school's yearbook. A further entry reads: "Sophomore Boy's Diary for Month of April...9. Fri. - Prof. Scott's Ag. class sowing their seeds 10. Sat. - Made garden all day...20. Tues. - Bawled out in Agriculture class for talking to A.N. Was shown the door....O.L. & T.H." (Otto Lance & Tola Hurlburt).
BENTON COUNTY HISTORICAL MUSEUM, HARRIET MOORE COLLECTION, 1982-004.

Above: Wagner's Restaurant, formerly located in the Masonic Building on the southwest corner of Third Street and Madison Avenue, ca. 1930. In 1927 Charles F. Wagner (pictured) bought out the bakery on this corner and changed the name to Wagner's Restaurant. He and his son, John, ran the restaurant. John continued to operate the business after his father's death from 1932 until 1968.

BENTON COUNTY HISTORICAL MUSEUM,
DORICE STEWART COLLECTION, 1991-118.0007.

Right: Building the foundation of the Benton County Courthouse in 1887 or 1888. Notice the columns of the 1850s courthouse in the upper left of the photograph. The old courthouse was moved to the north, and used while the new courthouse was being built. Scottish-born stonemason Thomas Mann (foreground) won the contract for building the foundation, doing the brickwork, and finishing the exterior. At $34,628, it was nearly half the project's cost.

HORNER MUSEUM COLLECTION, 989-2-13.

A PICTORIAL HISTORY
OF BENTON COUNTY

AT PLAY

HUNTING AND FISHING have played an important role in Benton County since early settlement. In the early days, these two activities were important sources of food for the family, but as time passed they became more sport-related. David Fagan's *History of Benton County* (1885) reports all kinds of animals were hunted, including whitetail deer, which, in the 1880s, was becoming increasingly rare. Fagan was concerned deer would become extinct because of "hounding over the country," where a dog was used to chase deer rather than as a "companion of the hunter, just to jump the deer...to give the hunter a fair shot." Bears and cougars were hunted, especially when they preyed on livestock. With continuing settlement of the valley floor, elk moved to the foothills of the Cascades and Coast Range, and were a more challenging quarry. Since the Willamette Valley is on the Pacific Flyway, ducks and geese were also hunted.

Fishing afforded a pleasurable and rewarding pastime as trout and "courser fish" were plentiful in the Willamette River, and salmon abounded in the Alsea River. Early settlers said,

when the salmon ran it looked as if "you could walk across the river on the backs of the fish."

During Alpine's spurt of growth in the early 20th century, it boasted two opera houses. The first was located above a drug store; when it was destroyed by fire, the second was built in an abandoned livery stable. A local artist painted the ceiling blue and added stars and a moon; the curtain was decorated in similar fashion. Traveling shows and local entertainers used the opera

Above: "Hiawatha" performed by students of Beaver Creek School in 1915 or 1916. Darrell Ebbert at far left.

BENTON COUNTY HISTORICAL MUSEUM, DARRELL EBBERT COLLECTION, 1999-018.0001.

house, and boxing matches were also held there. But Corvallis was the center for entertainment in the early days of Benton County settlement. In 1870 an opera house was built on the corner of Fourth and Madison streets using funds raised by Corvallis citizens who donated labor for its construction. The Opera House was used for dancing, city band performances, box socials, and even served as a skating rink. Still in use at the turn of the century for high school plays and other performances, the Opera House saw its demise, a result of the new moving pictures.

Despite being threatened with expulsion for rollerskating in 1876, students continued to skate, and it eventually became an acceptable pastime. In the early 1920s, Lake Park Roller Rink was built, named for the shallow lake excavated and diked next to the rink. Students not only skated in the rink, they also boated on the lake. During the 1930s, the members of the Civilian Conservation Corps living in nearby Camp Arboretum (now Peavy) used the facility, and during the Camp Adair era in the 1940s, it is reported that the rink was open around the clock. Use was so heavy during this period that a new floor had to be installed after the war.

Golf became very popular among the middle and upper classes in the early 20th century, and a Corvallis golf club was established in 1918. A visiting army officer indicated that sports helped take people's minds off the war and that golf was the best game for that. By 1924, there was a Corvallis Country Club complete with a golf course and clubhouse. Bowling also gained popularity with the opening of the Elite Bowling Alley in the new Weigand Building on NW Second in 1910—today, home of Peak Sports.

One of the recreational pursuits of the late 19th century was bicycling. In 1894, the Corvallis Cycling Club was organized. Around the turn of the century, the Corvallis and Albany bicycle clubs built a bike path between the two towns. It was located on the west side of present-day Highway 20.

Women's organizations such as the Corvallis Woman's Club and the Women's Christian Temperance Union provided not only social outlets for women but also a way to address their concerns about the community's social welfare. Men usually joined one of the local fraternal organizations or business clubs, which were often involved in community improvement projects.

Other popular offerings were riverboat excursions, train rides to the coast, and weekend camping trips to Sulphur Springs—located in what is now McDonald Forest. In her book, *Corvallis in 1900*, local historian Minerva Kiger Reynolds described Sunday excursions on the riverboats: "It was a most delightful trip—imagine floating down the Beautiful Willamette River with its banks tinted many colors with flowers and foliage….leaving Corvallis in the early morning and returning by moonlight. A delicious chicken dinner was served…and the Corvallis band went along and played…The fare…a dollar and half…"

In Corvallis, Chautauqua, a summer educational and entertainment program held in a large tent on the lower campus, drew big crowds. One person reported, "Everybody went; it was the thing to do." In Alpine the big Chautauqua tent was set up on the school grounds for "a week of entertainment inspirational and instructive."

It was becoming easier for people to go farther abroad for amusement. In the 1920s, especially with the completion of the Pacific Highway (U.S. 99) in 1923, automobile touring became popular. Many people built a second home at the coast or in an isolated mountain area. Others frequented "auto parks" along the new highway. The Auto Park at the City Park (Pioneer) in Corvallis was designated as one of the most inviting between Portland and San Diego. It featured camp ovens, tables, benches, a rest room with showers, a laundry room, and a main cabin with chairs, literature, and a phone. Electric lights illuminated the park, and if you didn't want to camp out, a row of connected cabins was provided. As the automobile became more and more a part of everyday life, more parks with campgrounds were made available around the county.

Bellfountain Park is Benton County's oldest public park. From 1851 until the turn of the 20th century it was used for religious camp meetings on the first Sunday in July—between haying and harvesting. These meetings were a time to renew old acquaintances, and perform marriages and baptisms. Religious revival meetings are still held in the park occasionally. In 1889, the first Corvallis City Park was established. The park was a gift from B.R. and Addie Job, and was designated "Franklin Square" by the City Council. Pioneer Park was the second park established; it was to be known as the "City Park and Fairgrounds"; however, the area was never developed as a fairgrounds. In 1927 a special election was held to approve a bond issue that would have allowed the purchase of land in the current location of Avery Park. Residents resoundingly defeated the proposal by a vote of 736 to 126, and the city did not purchase Avery Park until 1937.

Right: Oregon Agricultural College hiking party on Marys Peak, ca. 1920.
BENTON COUNTY HISTORICAL MUSEUM, FRANK GROVES COLLECTION, 1980-088.0020P.

Facing page: Corvallis firemen and Dalmatian relaxing on the southeast corner of Fourth Street and Madison Avenue. The bell behind the firemen is a monument erected in 1912 in memory of George P. Wrenn, Corvallis fireman who died while fighting a blaze at the W.A. Wells warehouse in 1882.
BENTON COUNTY HISTORICAL MUSEUM, HARRIET MOORE COLLECTION, 1982-004.0056P.

Above: Young Oregon Agricultural College professors at the end of a bicycle trip from San Francisco to Corvallis in 1896. Pictured are John Fulton, chemistry; E.G Emmatt, Mechanical Engineering; Fred W. Kent, dairy science; and D.W. Trine, botany. Taken at the S.B. Graham photograph studio.

Top: Playing pool at Wagner's pool hall. Charles Milton "Nap" Wagner behind the counter.
BENTON COUNTY HISTORICAL MUSEUM, DORICE STEWART COLLECTION, 1991-118.0006.

Below: Fishing on the Marys River. The dam in the photograph was located in what is now Avery Park. A dam in this location was erected in 1850 or 1851 to divert the waters of the Marys River for a mill race to power a sawmill, and later a gristmill, on the south side of the Marys near its confluence with the Willamette. Floods destroyed the dam several times. A dam is no longer in this location, but the mill race still exists.
BENTON COUNTY HISTORICAL MUSEUM, EDNA WIESE COLLECTION, 1990-068.1266.

Top: Harris Baseball Team, 1885. Scene looking west from the Harris Covered Bridge. First on left, Ed King. Fifth from left, Charlie Harris.

PHOTO COURTESY OF ELMER TAYLOR, WREN 4.

Middle: Playing baseball in Kings Valley in 1914.

BENTON COUNTY HISTORICAL MUSEUM,
MR. AND MRS. ANDREW AYERS COLLECTION, 1980-030.0032P.

Bottom: Ladies' foot race at the picnic for Corvallis Telephone Company employees.

BENTON COUNTY HISTORICAL MUSEUM, ARTHUR L. LOWE COLLECTION,
1999-128.0011.

Above: From left to right, Charles Madden, his son Gene Madden, and Joe Follet display their catch near Alsea, ca. 1940.

PHOTO SUBMITTED BY BARBARA METZGER, GT 25.

Above: Performance at the Corvallis Opera House, 1902. The Opera House was located on the southwest corner of Fourth Street and Madison Avenue.

BENTON COUNTY HISTORICAL MUSEUM, EDNA WIESE COLLECTION, 1990-068.1427.

Facing page top: Alsea Park, July 5, 1910. Party from Alpine/Bellfountain area. Pictured from left to right are: Angie Kyle, Clarence Aylesworth, Golda Howard, Golda's cousin from Kentucky, Preston Hammer, Ida Belknap, unidentified, Fult Woolridge, Merle Howard, and Bridge Woolridge.

PHOTO SUBMITTED BY JUDY ANN BUTLER, GT 6.

Facing page bottom: World War II soldiers playing baseball at Camp Adair. Although military training was the most important activity for the men at Camp Adair, there was time for recreation. Thousands of men trained at the camp. For a time it was the second largest city in Oregon. (U.S. ARMY SIGNAL CORPS PHOTOGRAPH)

BENTON COUNTY HISTORICAL MUSEUM, MARY LOU GREENE COLLECTION, 1993-041.0036.

ALSEA JULY 5 1910

Above: John B. and Isabelle Horner with their children Pearl and Vera bicycling in the 1890s.
HORNER MUSEUM COLLECTION, 980-72-3A.

Below: Corvallis Girls' Riding Club, 1914.
BENTON COUNTY HISTORICAL MUSEUM, CORVALLIS PUBLIC LIBRARY COLLECTION, 1985-032.0025BP.

Above: Playing cards inside the Woodcock house in Corvallis, early 1900s. Pictured from left to right are Clara Lane, Amanda Jane, Emma Jane and Arthur Roy Woodcock. The Woodcock house was on Fifth Street at the present location of the law enforcement building. The house was moved to Northeast Pilkington Lane in 1975.
PHOTO SUBMITTED BY LISA CURTIS, GT 10.

Below: Benton County champions, 1932. Monroe Union High School women's basketball team. Muriel Smith Gwellim, back left.
PHOTO SUBMITTED BY SUSAN FIELDS, GT 13.

Above: Community picnic at Sulphur Springs around 1919 or 1920. There was a camp-ground in an open field adjacent to the spring. People drank the spring water and bottled it for later use. The area wasn't used for recreation much after the 1920s.

PHOTO SUBMITTED BY VELMA RAWIE, GT 26.

Right: All-women party during World War I at a Women's Society Hall dance.

PHOTO SUBMITTED BY PATTI JANEGO, GT 18.